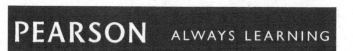

PEARSON ALWAYS LEARNING

Mike Southon • Chris West

The Beermat Entrepreneur
Turn Your Good Idea into a Great Business

with Contributions by Geoffery Malleck

Canadian Edition – Eh?

Taken from:
*The Beermat Entrepreneur: Turn Your
Good Idea into a Great Business*,
Revised Second Edition
by Mike Southon and Chris West

Pearson Learning Solutions, 501 Boylston Street, Suite 900, Boston, MA 02116
A Pearson Education Company
www.pearsoned.com

Printed in Canada

1 2 3 4 5 6 7 8 9 10 XXXX 17 16 15 14 13 12

000200010270780799

BK

ISBN 10: 1-256-92424-5
ISBN 13: 978-1-256-92424-1

Contents

Foreword

John Sleeman,
President,
Sleeman's Brewery

"When I was in high school and doing rather poorly, it seems that all I could think about was being in business for myself, instead of whatever the teachers had in mind for me that day. I wasn't really sure what kind of business; I just knew that I preferred the idea of building someTHING over the thought of working for someBODY. This was the late '60's and the word "entrepreneur" was used disparagingly more often than positively. As young men do, I would tell people of my dreams and as listeners often do, eyes would roll and I would be counseled to come back to the real world.

Unbelievably, my parents allowed me to drop out of school, maybe they just got tired of trying to get me to stop daydreaming & just do my homework. I bounced around from job to job, hoping that a bright light of inspiration would suddenly appear. I got married when I was a teenager and moved to England. Still no business spark but I did find the beer trade fun and interesting from a consumers' perspective, probably not the first guy to feel that way. Moving back to Canada, I was starting to focus my interest on the production & sales side and began thinking about building my pub, which then led to creating a beer importing company, which eventually saw us resurrecting the old Sleeman family brewery. All along the process I had questions, about myself, my abilities, how to make decisions, how to treat people, what to do when you run out of money, how to stay focused and on what, how to divide my time between my love of family & my passion for my business. I always had detractors, people who said "it can't be done". But I was fortunate in that my family supported my ideas and over the years equally fortunate that I have been able to surround myself with great people, both advisors and employees. But I was never able to find a book that would quickly give me hope and the answers to the situations that I'd find myself in. I was always in a hurry ... never enough time. The literature all seemed to be 500 pages long, spoken in a language that a high school dropout couldn't understand and frankly didn't address the concerns of a small start-up business. If I could have had a book like "The Beermat Entrepreneur" from the beginning, it might have helped me avoid feeling like my problems were unique to me, that I was going through things others had never experienced and who knows, as a result maybe I wouldn't have made some of my many mistakes.

This country needs home grown entrepreneurs, people who will stay in Canada, take risks, create employment, (and dare I say pay taxes?) and in turn encourage the next generation of young men and women to be leaders. The "Beermat Entrepreneur" will be a great aid in helping those people realize their dream and achieve that goal."

Best wishes,

John Sleeman

Founder and Chairman

Sleeman Breweries Ltd.

Foreword

Terry Campbell,
Chief Operating Officer,
Canadian Youth Business
Foundation (CYBF)

cybf.ca

Canada is a country rich in outstanding entrepreneurs. The economic value created by this talented and passionate group is astounding. With small- and medium-sized companies making up the bulk of our economy, our future depends not only on creating new businesses but also supporting their success.

The Canadian Youth Business Foundation (CYBF) understands that the entrepreneurial spirit and desire to create and grow a business requires a combination of talent, drive, vision, passion and a bit of luck. To be successful, emerging entrepreneurs need effective tools and great support networks that offer pre-launch coaching, business resources, start-up financing and mentoring, to help face the challenges involved in realizing their dreams.

This book offers passion and clarity to aspiring entrepreneurs. It provides practical, straightforward advice and is a one-stop "how-to" manual about getting a viable business off the ground. I would recommend it to anyone considering starting their own venture.

Preface to the revised edition

The success of *Beermat* was a delightful surprise, and I'd like to thank everyone who made it so – most of all, all the people who went out and bought the book! Chris and I have now been asked to prepare a revised second edition.

Looking back to the original versions, I'm delighted to see how little needs changing. We've met, and helped, many entrepreneurs and SMEs since *Beermat* appeared, and learnt a whole heap more in the process – a process that we hope will never end. But there are no areas of the original where we have found ourselves having to backtrack in a major way. A piece of fine-tuning here, a new distinction there ...

Oddly, the business environment has reverted to one similar to that in which the book first appeared back in 2002. Then we were all suffering hangovers from the great dotcom boom and bust. Now it's the credit crunch. In between, there has been a period of prosperity, and this will, of course, come again. But even in what appear to be 'bad' times, bright, motivated individuals – and groups of individuals – are founding businesses and prospering. There are always opportunities, especially for those enterprises that follow the Beermat route and avoid the blandishments of Big Capital. There is always 'pain' out there in the market – if you have a solution for that pain, which you can replicate and sell profitably, then now is the time to get your business started.

For us, the biggest change has been the development of the Beermat website, www.beermat.biz, which has been through a number of instantiations but now offers (we think, anyway) an unrivalled set of learning and networking tools for entrepreneurs (and it's fun). Come and visit us there.

As I said in the original version, this book is a team effort. The entrepreneurial experience is largely mine, hence the pronoun 'I' used throughout a book apparently written by two people. Chris brought his outstanding literary and journalistic skill, plus his own business experience, to the party. Rachael Stock at Pearson turned our manuscript into a fine book – and most importantly shared our passion for its message as she did so.

It doesn't stop there, of course. Many people looked at early drafts or editions and gave us the benefit of their knowledge and experience, which has enriched what you are about to read enormously. Thanks to Bill Thompson, who came up with the book's title (we'd been pondering this for weeks: it took Bill about five minutes); to Martin Rich and Erik Larsen at City University Business School; to (in alphabetical order) David Baynes, John Beevor, Christine Comaford-Lynch, Nick Fleisiak, Sir Campbell Fraser, Rachael Gonzalez, Gervas Huxley, Sally Jones, Simon Linford, Ian Masson, Rick Medlock, Graham Michelli, Jamie Mitchell, Nick Moreno, Steve Packard, Dev Patel, Stephen Pavlovitch, Guy Reavley, Carol Sarler, Peter Wallace, Chris Weller and Jim White.

Thanks also to everyone involved in The Instruction Set, both customers and employees, particularly the original 'Beermat Entrepreneur', Peter Griffiths, and the other cornerstones David Griffiths, Mike Banahan and Andy Rutter. Without you, I would probably still be selling scaffolding ...

A point on style. Our entrepreneur and team can be male or female. To use 'he' and 'his' all the time clearly fails to reflect this, but oscillating between 'he' and 'she' sounds odd, and endless repetitions of 'his or her' (or 'her or his') are just plain ugly. So we have mostly plumped for the 'singular they' – e.g. 'The entrepreneur and their team ...' Apologies to any purists. We also find the economists' mantra 'goods or services' rather ungainly, and prefer to talk of 'products'.

I'm always delighted to get comments from readers. Is there anything I have missed? What's *your* experience of founding and building a business? Can I help with any current business problems? Please get in touch with me at mike@beermat.biz or visit the website, at www.beermat.biz

Mike Southon, London, 2008

Why a Canadian Version, eh?

Since 1999 I have had the honour of teaching the principles of entrepreneurship at the University of Waterloo. Amongst other things *the University of Waterloo is recognized for its creative approach to education and for fostering of culture of innovation. For many, this is an opportunity to acquire knowledge and develop the skills, knowledge and attitudes to become innovators.*

A few years ago I began a search for a textbook that would compliment the objectives and principles of my course. The course has steadily evolved from that of a new venture creation course to a course that explores creativity leading to an innovation thus providing the foundation to launch an entrepreneurial venture. I have noticed that there are ample courses on starting businesses and writing business plans. What is lacking are courses that expose students to the benefits of disciplined creativity as a catalyst leading to the formation of an entrepreneurial venture.

Since the class delivery style better resembles a casual, storytelling (case) experience; with discussion intended to provoke the students; I wanted to avoid the more formal, research rich and word heavy texts that proliferate the various publisher libraries.

A second challenge is delivering business material to non-business students. The aforementioned texts simply miss the mark by not offering the specific information in a language that aligns with my course. It is not that they are bad, just inappropriate for my audience. I needed a resource that addressed the class in a similar way to my own approach; namely, to offer a basic context for entrepreneurship while presenting it as a viable and attractive option for the right person. I wanted a book that could be read on a Saturday afternoon for pleasure and not because it had to be read. I wanted a book that would be lent to friends. Now I am not criticizing the other excellent textbooks available. Each is well conceived and provides ample information, but I wanted something different.

So I contacted the publisher's marketing representatives and put out the challenge to find a book that meets these conditions. Pearson contacted me a couple of weeks later suggesting such a book is available but warning me that it is a British text and most examples (and some lingo) are uniquely British. After spending a very pleasant evening reading the book with an unusual title (what is a Beermat anyway?) ... well you know what happened next.

Since adapting the Beermat Entrepreneur into my class, thousands of students have enjoyed being guided by the comfortable, inspiring and 'bang-on' text. Even more compelling is the fact that these students have shared the Beermat with friends or kept as part of their library. I was both surprised and delighted to see a copy on the bookshelf in my son and daughter-in-law's home. You see, before she knew my son, Lindsay took my course. Since taking my course she has shared the book with family and friends. The book remains a part of their library. My son chose well.

In the University of Waterloo community sightings of the Beermat Entrepreneur have been witnessed at our local business accelerators, in the various entrepreneurship related campus clubs, on the desks of the fledging start ups and in the hands of capital providers and mentors. The Beermat is useful without being overbearing and debilitating. It provides valuable information that can be applied in the three distinct stages in the life of an enterprise. The Beermat represents the beginning of knowledge acquisition for the aspiring entrepreneur.

The *Canadianization* of the Beermat Entrepreneur will not change the feel or the instructions provided by authors Southon and West. The goal is to simply replace some of the cases with Canadian equivalents and modify some terminology (what is a lift?).

I have always been confident in my decision to use the Beermat and that the text created by authors Southon and West has been an important part of my classroom experience. Thanks to them for what remains an inspiring guide.

Lastly ... a quick note for the naysayers who cry foul by claiming you cannot teach entrepreneurship: Frankly, you are correct! My course does not turn students into entrepreneurs. I liken my course to an art course, which cannot take credit for creating the artist. Both awaken the need to express one's creativity. My course shows the precarious and adventure-rich lifestyle that is the entrepreneur. It provides a sense of the potential satisfaction for individuals possessing the right stuff to venture forward. My goal is to ignite the interest in enough students to consider the lifestyle of entrepreneurship, thereby ensuring continued prosperity for our nation.

Geoff Malleck, 2012

Introduction

Why 'The Beermat Entrepreneur'?

In the original British version of the Beermat Entrepreneur the authors describe how an evening at the local pub lead to the creation of their successful enterprise, 'The Instruction Set'. Often the playful banter of a couple of friends trying to figure out a better way of doing things or debating on how to solve a problem may lead to the creation of an enterprise. While it is only a first of many steps, it is still that important first of many steps. For the authors, the concept of what would become the Instruction Set was scribbled onto a 'beermat' or what we refer to in Canada as a 'coaster'. It is for this reason that the title was applied to the book.

History is littered with enterprises that were conceived in comparable ways. The starting point of a very successful airline was conceived by sketching the unique strategy onto a cocktail napkin. From Success magazine comes this description, "An opportunity presented itself for Herb Kelleher in 1966. One of his clients, Rollin King, owned a small commuter air service in San Antonio. King and his banker, John Parker, dreamed up the Southwest Airlines concept as a cheaper, more convenient way to travel between Houston, Dallas and San Antonio—cities more than 200 miles apart. King pitched the idea to Kelleher, and during discussions over drinks, a triangle between those cities—sketched on a cocktail napkin—became the company's first paperwork."
http://www.success.com/articles/390-from-the-corner-office-herb-kelleher

In Canada, one of the world's most successful leisure games was also conceived by a couple of friends who, at a bar, decided they could invent a better board game.

There is a natural tendency to complain about things and how you would solve them. Sometimes those creative moments lead to amazing outcomes. Take, for instance, a couple of friends who met at a local pub to play 'Scrabble' and went on to imagine a board game that they would really like to play. From that evolved one of the most successful board games in recent history as Chris Haney and Scott Abbott took their roughly drawn placement sketches and introduced the world to Trivial Pursuit.

In December 1993, Trivial Pursuit was named to the "Games Hall of Fame" by Games magazine.

(Adapted from, "The History of Trivial Pursuit was invented by Canadians, Chris Haney and Scott Abbott. Bellis, Mary) http://www.canada.com/life/Trivial+Pursuit+creator+Chris+ Haney+dead/3093782/story.html#ixzz1xD0vrbfX

Worth watching: CBC Video http://www.cbc.ca/archives/categories/economy-business/ consumer-goods/the-joy-of-toys-and-games/invention-of-trivial- pursuit.html

As expressed in class, almost as a plea, to my students is the need for them to engage in debate, to challenge each other, to embrace dialogue, and to find joy in a hearty argument. I tread carefully by suggesting they trade in the typical Thursday evening of loud music and bright lights for a more subdued evening at a quiet pub. Conversation is often the spark that leads to creativity and from there; who knows where it may lead ...

The authors of the Beermat entered the world of business during the great dotcom boom and bust. This was a great lesson in how not to do business. What went terribly wrong in the technology sector in the late 1990's ...

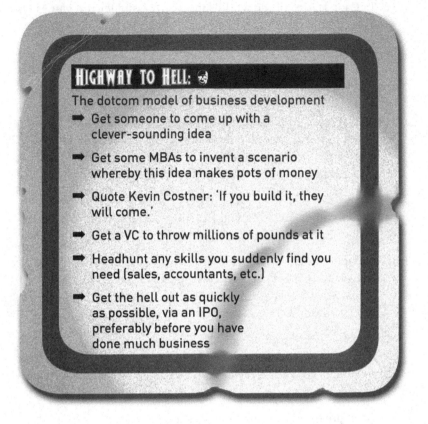

HIGHWAY TO HELL:

The dotcom model of business development

➡ Get someone to come up with a clever-sounding idea

➡ Get some MBAs to invent a scenario whereby this idea makes pots of money

➡ Quote Kevin Costner: 'If you build it, they will come.'

➡ Get a VC to throw millions of pounds at it

➡ Headhunt any skills you suddenly find you need (sales, accountants, etc.)

➡ Get the hell out as quickly as possible, via an IPO, preferably before you have done much business

It would be a bad case of history repeating itself if you were going to make any of these assumptions or apply any of these tactics. It was and will remain ... dumb.

Business is easy

It annoys some people when I say that business is easy. But it's true. Almost all the business screw ups I have seen, and I've seen plenty, have been due to people getting very simple things wrong.

66 Success in business involves *hard work*. Lots of it, twenty-hours-a-day-for-five years hard work. 99

Of course, success in business involves *hard work*. Lots of it, twenty-hours-a-day-for-five-years hard work. But if you love business, you're up for that. With the right people and the right motivation, you'll enjoy it most of the time (not all the time – business is not that easy).

Note the caveat 'if you love business'. If you don't get a buzz from business – the ideas, the technology, the people – you really shouldn't go near a start-up. Or any commercial organization, really. Scale down your financial ambitions and find another way of making a living and of making a difference to the world.

Business also involves making *hard choices* – not often, but occasionally. But these choices are usually not as hard as they look. You usually know in your heart what you have to do; it's just a matter of summoning up the willpower.

Success also requires a measure of *luck* – but as the golfer Gary Player said, 'The harder I practice the luckier I get'.

Most of all, though, I believe that success in business means *following the right pattern*. This is what this book is about: a pattern that begins with self-examination and grows naturally from there, potentially to a point where you are leading an organization that affects the lives of thousands of people: customers, employees, shareholders ...

A successful business is a living thing. So like all living things, it has a natural pattern of growth. You ignore this pattern at your peril, just as if you fail to repot seedlings at the right time they'll die, or if you plant a sapling in the wrong kind of soil you'll soon be confronted with a dead-looking stick instead of that riot of colour that you saw at the garden centre.

Some people baulk at this talk of patterns. Isn't business about flair and imagination? Isn't business an art as much as a science? The great entrepreneurs didn't sit around studying theory, any more than Monet and Rembrandt went out and bought those kits where you dab paint into little numbered sections ...

I can only say that the more I see businesses fail or succeed, the more I believe that there is a pattern to their growth that has to be worked with to ensure success, and that I understand this pattern well enough to start telling other people about it.

There is, perhaps, an analogy with the way that scriptwriting is taught in Hollywood. There are strict rules for developing plots, rules which compel attention and which make stories work. But they do not of themselves guarantee success: if they are followed without flair, the results are leaden (though still adequate: DVD rental places are full of them). You need aptitude *as well* as rules to excel.

Which is why you must begin your journey to business success by asking ...

Where do I fit in?

The popular vision of a growing company is of a group of followers flocking round the banner of a charismatic entrepreneur/ leader. The reality is much subtler than this. Yes, there will be a classic Gerald Schwartz or Peter Munk figure at the centre of things, but they are not the whole story. Or even half of it. There are concentric rings of very special people around every entrepreneur, without whom the business will go nowhere, without whom the entrepreneur will just spend their days dreaming or impressing people in pubs.

This book is for entrepreneurs, but also for the people who form these concentric rings, who are *just as important* as entrepreneurs. These people are not – and this is where many businesses go wrong – passive sidekicks, but key players in their own right.

For any individual wanting to work in an entrepreneurial environment, the first question must be: 'What role am I best suited to play?'

The entrepreneur ...

Entrepreneurs are, for all their faults (see below), very special people. Are you one? Look in this mirror and be honest: is the face staring back yours?

Entrepreneurs are *confident*. They're born optimists, they simply know they can do it. This optimism is often irrational; it can infuriate their more realistic friends, but it just bubbles up in them. 'I can do it!' And they *will* do it, as well. It's not that they don't feel fear – all sane people do – but when push comes to shove, their confidence just steamrollers over the fear and they get on with what needs to be done.

Entrepreneurs are also *charismatic*. They inspire people. They're not just optimistic, they have optimism to spare, optimism which they radiate and instill in others around them. No wonder they attract people, not just sheep but energetic, imaginative winners. They'll need this quality, over and over again – with their business partners, with their employees, with their sources of finance, most important of all with their customers. But that's fine, as they've got a seemingly endless supply of it.

"Entrepreneurs are *confident*. They're born optimists, they simply *know* they can do it."

I've seen a few apparent exceptions to this, but on closer examination, entrepreneurs all have charisma in the right circumstances. Bill Gates, for example, seems to lack this quality – to the general public. But I saw him years ago among a group of techies, and the man was a magnet.

Entrepreneurs have bags of *energy*. They're going to need it, every ounce of it. But somehow, they know it's there. All the entrepreneurs I have met seem to sleep less than normal.

Entrepreneurs are *obsessed with work*. They talk about it all the time. Not the best thing at parties, but it does make for success.

Entrepreneurs are *ambitious*. Obvious, you might say, but it's an essential part of the make-up. Ambition on its own, however, does not make an entrepreneur. A generalized ambition – 'I want to be rich' – isn't enough, either. The entrepreneur's ambition is about *wanting to change things* and about knowing they have the wherewithal to make this change. What they change can be anything, from how clothes are sourced to a highly technical software application. Whatever, it sucks at the moment, and the entrepreneur is going to change it.

Entrepreneurs are *in a hurry*. Not only are they going to change things, they are going to change things fast.

In the classroom I have used four different terms (with examples) to describe the entrepreneur. I use these terms for two reasons. The first is the appropriateness of the word. The second is that these are terms often considered undesirable from a societal perspective. The first word is disruptive. Entrepreneurs seek large-scale change. In short, disruptive entrepreneurs seek revolution.

The second is irrational. It is the ability to see things from a different perspective, to capture trends not yet formed in the minds of others, to challenge convention, to find opportunity where others see only mistakes.

The third word is unreasonable. George Bernard Shaw expressed this point best when he stated, "The reasonable man adapts himself to the world; the unreasonable man persists in trying to adapt the world to himself. Therefore all progress depends on the unreasonable man."

The fourth preferred term describing the entrepreneur is curious. Curiosity is the catalyst that drives the entrepreneur to wonder, to consider, to challenge, to improve and to invent. Einstein is quoted as saying, "I have not special talent. I am only passionately curious."

Does this look like you? Great.

Now for the difficult part.

Entrepreneurs are also *arrogant*. They know they are good. At everything. With a strong team around them – and they can't flourish without such a team – this attitude mellows to 'I'm good at everything. But I don't have the time to do everything, so I have to let the people in finance, sales, delivery and so on get on with it.' But even then, the team need to remain on guard against the entrepreneur's passion for meddling. The worst thing about this meddling is that it is appallingly inconsistent. One day the entrepreneur will be stomping round the office fixing light bulbs, the next phoning up customers out of the blue, the next trying to rewrite software, the next ...

This arrogance is the 'flip' side of the entrepreneur's confidence and vision. Vision is not always a good trait: Hitler and Stalin 'knew they were right'. But then so did Winston Churchill and Mother Teresa.

They are also *manipulative*. Just as arrogance is the flip side of the entrepreneur's confidence and vision, manipulation is the dark side of charisma. Entrepreneurs use people. They may inspire them, they may pay them well, they may enable them to achieve things they'd never achieve on their own – but they still use people.

Entrepreneurs *can't complete things*. They're forever coming up with new ideas. They love brainstorming sessions; they blaze with excitement at new projects. 'Why don't we ...' 'Supposing ...' 'And then we can ...'

This inability to complete things is perhaps part of a bigger weakness – *lack of focus*. I said that entrepreneurs are obsessed with work, and they are. Yet at the same time they seem unable to focus on specific issues for any length of time. It's as if, having isolated themselves from most of what the rest of us call life, they have to pace round and round this little courtyard with extra energy. If you are an entrepreneur, please make yourself focus on detail. More important, listen to your closest colleagues when *they* focus on detail.

"If you are an entrepreneur, please make yourself focus on detail. More important, listen to your closest colleagues when *they* focus on detail."

Entrepreneurs can become *obsessed with the competition*. I actually know one who founded a company with the sole purpose of put-

ting a rival out of business. I shall talk about 'how to compete' later, but I don't think I'm giving too much away by saying this obsession can be disastrous, both commercially and personally. If you feel yourself going down this road – don't. Concentrate on improving *your* proposition. You don't win the golf game by focusing on the opponent's ball.

Entrepreneurs can be *impatient*. Throughout this book, I talk about the 'hurdles' that an idea has to jump in order to succeed. You can't miss these out and charge straight for the finishing line.

So there we have it. Mature, sophisticated, gentle? No. Childish, obsessive, ruthless – that's more like it. More like you?

I don't want to end this section on a negative note. Successful entrepreneurs create employment, opportunities, choice, wealth. They inspire people to do things of which they hardly imagined themselves capable. They challenge orthodoxy and change society much more than most politicians ever do. If it weren't for these men and women of vision – with all their weaknesses – we'd probably still be sitting around in caves.

Entrepreneurs truly change the world.

But they don't do so alone.

... and their teams

It's clear from the above that the lone entrepreneur is not going to found, let alone run, a successful business. They'll lose interest too soon, they'll miss crucial details, they'll alienate key stakeholders – they'll be back in the pub again in no time, drawing another idea on another beermat.

They need a team around them.

Actually they need two teams, a 'founding' team and a 'dream' team. These build at different stages of the business' growth. In its first stage, when the enterprise is still a seedling, the entrepreneur will need a group of four people around them. Four cornerstones, on which the business will be built. Later, when the enterprise grows to a sapling, 15 more people will be required: lively, passionate, committed team players, like the sporting 'dream team'.

The four cornerstones

The engine room – and often the totality – of a start-up company is the entrepreneur, plus their four closest associates, the four cornerstones. The image that comes to mind is of a pyramid, with the entrepreneur at the apex and four rock-solid supports beneath them.

I shall talk about what the cornerstones actually do later – at the moment, I am concerned with what sort of people they are.

The answer is a very special mixture of solidity and entrepreneurial passion.

Their *solidity* comes from their commercial or technical discipline. Cornerstones are professionals – at sales, finance, technology or delivery. This expertise and professionalism provides essential objectivity. Objectivity is something entrepreneurs need badly, though they are usually in blissful ignorance of that need.

"Cornerstones are nearly as *passionate* about the venture as the entrepreneur is."

At the same time, cornerstones are not there just to pour cold water over the entrepreneur. They are nearly as *passionate* about the venture as the entrepreneur is. Sometimes, when the entrepreneur is in a sulk because some part of their dream isn't working out, the cornerstones are more passionate. But they never lose their objectivity, their priceless gift of perspective.

Cornerstones also have considerable *personal skills*. It's not enough just to be passionate about the idea and good at a business discipline. Working with the mercurial entrepreneur, cornerstones need to be able to tell the truth tactfully, and to remain calm and cool when the entrepreneur still tries to over-rule them.

They need the entrepreneur's capacity for *hard work* – there are no free rides in a new business.

They also need *courage*: probably more courage than the entre-preneur even, as entrepreneurs are driven by their vision, while cornerstones can see the potential hazards much more clearly.

Finally, cornerstones are *doers*; you give them a job and they get it done, whatever the obstacles.

There's one of those acronyms here. What you need in a corner-stone is lots of SPPHCD (solidity, passion, personal skills, hard work, courage and doers)! I hate acronyms.

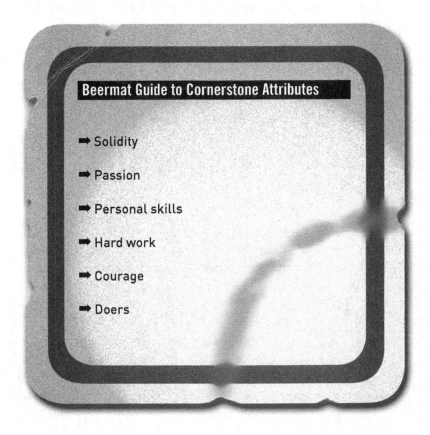

Beermat Guide to Cornerstone Attributes

➡ Solidity

➡ Passion

➡ Personal skills

➡ Hard work

➡ Courage

➡ Doers

In many businesses, one of the cornerstones is a 'foil' to the entrepreneur. This person plays a quieter role, providing some key technical skill – often finance – but also talking ideas through with the entrepreneur. Ray Kroc, who had the vision to turn the McDonald brothers' hamburger joint into an international success story owes a great deal to his financial manager, Harry Sonneborn. Harry was the individual who designed the financial model that turned an organization making very little money into a hugely profitable firm. Jim Balsille did this for Mike Lazaridis in the process of turning Research in Motion into a global success story.

Please note that the cornerstones do not have to be, and should not be, full-time from day one.

The four cornerstones' qualities will make the difference between the new company's success and failure. They will do so when the company is tiny; they will do so later, when they use these skills to manage not only the entrepreneur but also a growing number of subordinates.

The dream team

When the business expands further, a wider set of supports will be needed. I talk about this 'dream team' in the chapter on the

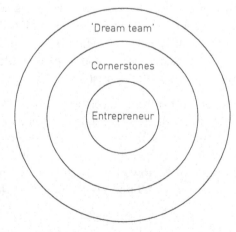

The entrepreneur and their teams

sapling enterprise. This second, outer ring of people is still very special. Like cornerstones, they are a mixture of solid commercial/technical skill and entrepreneurial flair: probably the main difference between them and the cornerstones is their level of skill and experience, which will be a little lower. They will be passionate and imaginative and, above all, team players, hence the allusion to dream teams in sport.

The intrapreneur

Do you work for a big company but secretly dream of being an entrepreneur? Do you at the same time fear the loss of security that would come from packing the job in and 'going it alone'? I have met plenty of people in this situation.

The way forward is to become an 'intrapreneur' – to set up (or join) an entrepreneurial division within your company. As the marketplace becomes ever more competitive and fast-moving, more and more businesses are setting up such divisions. They are right to be doing so and, if your employer is not, you could be doing them – and yourself – a big favour by getting them on to this bandwagon.

The classic model of the enterprise division is the Apple 'skunkworks', complete with Jolly Roger over their outbuildings. They saved the company, which was throwing money at an over-specified machine called the Lisa, by developing the Macintosh. The boss of the skunkworks, Steve Jobs, then left the company – which began to drift again. Only when he returned, hoisted the Skull and Crossbones once more, and came up with products like the iMac, did Apple begin to flourish again.

The story of the Post-it note, developed inside the 3M company by Arthur Fry, is another classic: fed up with page markers that kept falling out of his hymnbook, Fry developed a marker backed with a 'failed' experimental glue – a glue that had been rejected because of its low sticking power. He presented the idea to his superiors, who politely sidelined it. He made some prototypes and gave them to the secretaries in his office, who soon found them indispensable. The bosses noticed ...

In both these cases, the 'intrapreneur' had to fight hard for their product against a sceptical corporate bureaucracy, and this is often the case. Intrapreneurism is not a soft option. It seems that intrapreneurs are the most likely to be fired in many organizations. They simply cannot accept convention- they must challenge it. This doesn't always sit well with those seeking conformity or mediocrity.

However, it does have some advantages over the traditional start-up. The mother company can provide things such as premises, funding and contacts that the entrepreneur has to fight for. But the fundamental process of building an enterprise is the same within a company as outside it, so intrapreneurs should read this book and follow it as closely as entrepreneurs in the wicked world out there.

❝Intrapreneurism is not a soft option.❞

Note that, for companies, letting intrapreneurs loose is not a 'pure win' – there will be some downside. Remember those negative attributes of entrepreneurs: you are just about to unleash these people on your nice corporate culture. Some valuable, solid team players may be offended by their unconventional attitudes and buccaneering style. Of course, I think you've done the right thing – you're getting back to being a proper business again, not a Jurassic bureaucracy. But watch out for a few internal bruises.

Intrapreneurship is a huge topic, which I can only touch upon in this book.

Private life: a warning

Setting up and running a business is about as demanding an activity as you can get. If you are in a relationship – it may not survive the competition. If you already have a family – think very carefully about how you are going to balance out your time.

Entrepreneurs and cornerstones often tell their long-suffering partners 'I'm doing this to make us rich'. This is at best a half-truth. You're doing this because you need to, somewhere deep within you. Money is only a part of the reward. Some partners may resent this: 'You have me, why do you need this business as well?' Talk these issues through.

If you have kids, then the issue gets more serious still. I'm not saying don't start a business – and if I did, and you were a natural entrepreneur, you wouldn't listen anyway – but work this out. Talk to your partner.

You can forget that much-loved hobby, of course.

Other sacrifices may include your health (90 hour work weeks are not conducive to better health), your friendships, your spiritual journey, your favourite pastimes. You need to measure opportunity cost before venturing forward. It is much better to make these decisions early on. You must honestly measure the trade-off involved in starting a business.

So you've done this, and you're ready to go. And you were honest about yourself and so really know what role suits you best. Entrepreneur? Cornerstone? Dream team player? Intrapreneur?

The adventure starts here.

The
seedling
enterprise

SLEEMAN

NOTORIOUSLY GOOD

SINCE 1834

SLEEMAN.CA

There are three essential stages that a business passes through on its way to maturity. These stages are radically different from one another – in culture, in people, in management style, in finance, in selling ... In everything, really.

So different and distinct are these stages, that I nearly chose the image of a butterfly, whose larval, pupal and free-flying phases are totally unrecognizable as being related to the same creature. But there is a little more continuity than this – and anyway, will the massive company you eventually build really resemble one of those beautiful but evanescent creatures that flaps across your garden on a summer's day (till the cat attacks it)? I prefer the image of an oak: mighty, spreading, long-lasting ...

But your oak is a long way away yet. Right now, all we have is a simple acorn.

A good idea

The authors share a story in a pub. In this story the entrepreneur was coming up with ideas and two friends were listening ... The trouble with this situation is that it happens too often: entrepreneurs are forever bubbling over with ideas. What you need are not ideas, but *good* ideas, ones that really will grow into thriving businesses.

"What you need are not ideas, but *good* ideas, ones that really will grow into thriving businesses."

Where do the really good ideas come from, and how do you know them when they crop up?

Where do they come from? In my view, the answer is personal experience.

- A sales person knows their customers have been crying out for a widget that does X, but nobody's making one at the moment.
- A technical expert is convinced that there's a way to write software that does Y (or that does good old Z much cheaper ...).
- A consumer is fed up with the poor standard of service in a particular area.

In all cases, the entrepreneur has asked a magic question: 'Where's the pain?' Business ideas which don't salve pain run the risk of becoming solutions in search of problems.

Great business ideas often centre on a disruptive idea or on a market *dislocation*. I define a dislocation as a change that radically alters the way people do things. In other words, not 'the same thing but a bit better', but a totally new practice. In the introduction I defined this as being disruptive. In reality, the dividing line between improvement and disruptive is fuzzy. Clearly the latest 'improved' version of a washing powder lies on one side of this line, and a totally new sociological phenomenon like the Internet lies on the other. I would put the Blackberry by Research in Motion on the disruptive side, because it changed the way people communicated and transacted. This was part of a massive sociological upheaval, but a small but real change. By contrast, the Canadian designed IMAX experience involved revolutionary technology but was still a movie experience (it enhanced an existing experience): it belongs on the 'improvement' side.

It is one of the joys of market dislocations that they tend to come from left-field. Futurologists, city analysts and so on are busy at (and highly paid for) predicting market changes, and they almost always get it wrong. Steven Covey referred to a quote by the president and founder of Digital Equipment in 1977 who said, *"There is no reason for any individual to have a computer in their home."*

Or what about the talent scout at Decca Records who listened to The Beatles' demo and said that the days of groups with guitars were over?

Back to the Blackberry reference, advances like text messaging seem to come from nowhere. The experts in the telecom business said it would replace pagers. They did not predict it would change the way teenagers communicate, which it did, creating a whole new market for associated products like 'bbms' or applications including downloadable ring tones.

The relevance of this to the entrepreneur is that they should be keeping a very keen lookout for these dislocations.

Note that you do not have to *cause* the dislocations. Most entrepreneurs ride piggyback on dislocations – and thrive. Even a vast company like Cisco is still only a beneficiary of the Internet dislocation, not its cause. *You don't have to instigate total, radical change to build an entrepreneurial business.* What you do need is to have a sharp eye for how things are going – especially when customer needs or behaviours are changing fast – and a real ability to make products to suit that change. 'In the future, there's going to be a real need for X; we will deliver it, and this is how ...'

In our experience, entrepreneurs 'on the street' are never short of ideas. If you are reading this and thinking, 'I'd like to run my own business, but I can't think of what to do', you are not ready. Wait till you are seized by a furious determination to do something better than it's being done at the moment (and an insight into how you could do it better). Alternatively, check out franchise models, which will solve this problem for you.

"You don't have to instigate total, radical change to build an entrepreneurial business.**"**

How do you spot the winner? The answer to this, sadly, is 'you can't'. You only know the true mettle of an idea once you test it. People are always approaching us with ideas, asking what we think of them. Our reply is always that we don't know: it sounds fine, but only the market can give a valid verdict.

What we can say is that there are a number of clear *hurdles* that the idea will have to jump.

The first one is simply there, in the pub. If the entrepreneur's friends light up and someone says, 'Now that is a brilliant idea!', you have a small but real confirmation. Intuition is at work.

A second hurdle is next morning, when you wake up. In the clear light of day – and of sobriety – is it really such a good idea?

You should have decided the night before to go away and do a little research on the idea. If you are potential cornerstones, you will do this – not because you read it in this book, but because your curiosity and professional pride will make you do so anyway. If you're in sales, you'll float the idea across customers, not trumpeting it from the rooftops, but as an aside. If you're a techie, you'll knock up a prototype. If your forte is more delivery, you'll notice an ad in the paper offering cheap factory space.

Gather again, and compare notes. Are you still excited? Great. A third hurdle has been cleared.

Now is the time to draw up your first business plan. Unlike those business plans the size of telephone books that some 'experts' tell you to write, this plan is simple – so simple that you can write it down on the back of a beermat. It has three things on it, shown overleaf.

We call this plan your Original Beermat. It is, in its quiet way, a hugely powerful business tool.

Your elevator pitch

The elevator pitch, for those unfamiliar with the term, is what you would say to a potential investor, mentor or critical first customer if you found yourself in an elevator with him or her. I've heard, and still hear, too many so-called elevator pitches that seem to last forever – please, if you are approaching me, or anyone else, with an elevator pitch, stick to the rules. The Beermat elevator pitch is only two sentences long: the *premise* and the *endorsement*.

At the moment your idea has no endorsement, so work on the premise. A one-sentence description of your product's unique benefits. 'Clothes with a conscience' made in safe factories by people paid fair wages. Friction-free widgets. A new kind of screen for 3G mobile phones. Dedicated software for market-gardeners (the best elevator pitches also give some idea of your market).

The greatest elevator pitch premises are hugely evocative:

- Bill Gates' own: 'Enable everyone to harness the power of personal computing'.
- Federal Express's Fred Smith: 'Peace of Mind'.
- Montagu Burton: 'A three-piece suit for a week's wage'.
- Nike: 'Authentic Athletic Performance'.
- John D. Rockefeller at Standard Oil: 'Let the poor man have his cheap light'.

The elevator pitch premise should become a mantra for the people in your organization: the automatic, and natural-sounding, answer when anyone asks what the company does. So start now, by agreeing on a sentence that sums up the unique benefits the idea will bring to its customers.

Note that the idea is still only a fraction of the way along the obstacle course that will be its journey to commercial success. The idea doesn't have to be perfect here, just good enough. It will grow and change as you develop it, especially once you start talking to potential (and later, actual) customers. Your elevator pitch will change. Do your best for now, and never change it without a lot of thought.

The job of the endorsement is to lend some credibility to the premise, and thus convince Bill, or whoever you meet in the elevator, to take you seriously. Initially it will be the name of a person or company who are already taking you seriously; later, once you have proved you can do what you say, it will probably be your differentiator – the actual reason why people should buy from you rather than someone else.

Which brings me nicely on to the next item on the Beermat ...

Your mentor

Mentoring gets a passing mention in some of the books on entrepreneurial practice, but I believe it is a real key to success.

Hewlett-Packard famously started in a garage: it probably would have stayed there if it hadn't been for the mentorship of Fred Terman, founder of Stanford Research Park.

Heather Reisman CEO of Indigo Books and Music "My best business advice ever comes from Gerry (her husband entrepreneur Gerald Schwartz). When it comes to negotiating transactions, there is nobody on the planet like him," she says. She credits Schwartz with "enabling" her bookstore business, but not for the reasons that some observers assume. "Some people might say because he is rich I can do things," she laughs. "That has had almost no impact on my career because I built each business with money that I earned or raised. It is his judgment, support and perspective as an entrepreneur that I am the beneficiary of." http://www.theglobeandmail.com/report-on-business/rob-magazine/top-1000/inside-the-kobo-deal-that-netted-indigo-165-million/article4256906/?page=all

Now you're over that third hurdle, the next thing you must do is find a mentor.

You are looking for someone with huge experience of business, who gets the point of what you're doing, who likes you and whom you like.

I'll expand on these 'qualifications' below, but right now I expect you are already imagining objections. I did, when I first heard people talking about mentorship – but in retrospect, my objections were all wrong. You're in the pub: what do people say to this idea?

➡ *'Impossible – we don't know anyone like that'*
The second part of this objection may well be true. One of the aims of this book is to map out a path to success for *anybody* with an entrepreneurial mindset, whatever their current status or background. So maybe you're sitting here now and none of you knows anyone who falls into the category of potential mentor or anybody remotely like that.

Relax. Finding a mentor is not impossible, it is simply a matter of will. If you make it a priority, and I'm saying that you *must* make it a priority, then you can find a mentor. In the process you will learn a lesson, which will prove of use again and again in all phases of business: the importance of making and pursuing priorities.

Of course, it's easier to find a mentor if you're incredibly posh. If you have family that has a close connection with the chairman of the Royal Bank of Canada then clearly you have an advantage that few have.

If you work in a particular industry you should have some idea of who the 'elders' of that industry are. If not, get such an idea, fast. Maybe you have met one or some of these people in the course of your work. So approach them. True 'elders' are usually happy to be approached by genuinely enthusiastic people with genuinely decent ideas.

"True 'elders' are usually happy to be approached by genuinely enthusiastic people with genuinely decent ideas."

If there is nobody in your sector, try adjacent business sectors. The qualities for mentorship do not include 'works in your sector': at the highest level, skill, thinking and contacts range across all types of business.

If you are starting from a very low base in terms of your current work – unemployed or very junior – it is harder to find a mentor of requisite quality. But not impossible. Set about your search slowly, systematically, imaginatively. All communities have leaders of various kinds. Who runs the Chamber of Commerce in your town? Your local religious leader may have a wealth of contacts you didn't know about. Check out institutions like The Canadian Youth Business Foundation (cybf.ca) which has an excellent mentoring system (see Appendix B). Ask yourself: 'Among people I can talk to, who do I respect the most?'

Students have no excuse for not finding a mentor. Don't be afraid to approach a professor or instructor. Usually they do have an interest in your success. Try to get an interview with your president or vice-chancellor, who, if they care about their post (and most of them do) will be delighted to help enterprise within 'their' college or university.

In passing, if you are a student (or fresh out of school and raring to get your business moving), it might be an idea to spend a couple of years in the business you intend to shake up so radically – not to have the radicalism knocked out of you, but to hone and temper it. Watch what people do: there'll be some good stuff you didn't know about. Make contacts. Start looking for potential cornerstones. Get closer to the movers and shakers in the industry. Give yourself a yardstick for when you run your own business (even if it's 'We're so much better than those people I worked for at ABC'). And, of course, let someone else pay the bill while you make early mistakes.

'First-step' people (local religious leader, college tutor) will not be mentors themselves, but they will know people who might be, or who (in turn) know people who might be. If you approach these people with seriousness and enthusiasm, they will move you towards the right person.

If you are *still* stuck for ideas, think of who has written a business book you really admire or think of a business you really admire, and find out who the directors are. A hint here is to avoid the obvious names: Jim Pattison probably gets hundreds of ideas fired at him every day, but there are plenty of potentially superb mentors on boards of great companies for whom the experience would be refreshing.

➡ *'I don't want to deal with a load of old farts.'*
Someone will say that. Someone who's quite fun but a bit immature, probably. It's time they grew up, and started taking people of all ages for what they are. The adventure of business success challenges everybody's preconceptions – class, sex, age, race. That's one of the purposes of pursuing it.

➡ *'Supposing they nick the idea?'*
This is an understandable fear, but grossly overrated. When I worked at a launch network, almost all the entrepreneurs I met

wanted me to sign a non-disclosure agreement before they would let me read their business plan. I used to explain that success is about having a good idea *and putting it into practice*. Even the cleverest ideas are ten-a-penny. (It was company policy not to sign such agreements anyway, on the basis of our professional integrity.)

Once your idea is up and running and making money, then people will try to copy it. But don't worry about that now (or ever, really – see later).

People who've made it to the top know this. They are also people who enjoy the business of putting ideas into practice. If they like your idea, they'll be excited by the prospect of helping you make it work, not by the prospect of pinching it.

➡ *'People like that won't listen to us'*
'People at the top of businesses are bastards. They have to be, to get and stay there. They won't want to waste their time listening to wannabes ...'

That is an urban myth.

Clearly there are a few very unpleasant people at the top of businesses – sadly some of them are entrepreneurs – but most of the top people I have met, and I've met lots, have been very nice. This is largely because they have to be, in order to get and keep good people to work for and with them.

➡ *'OK – but I don't know what to say to someone that important'*
Be yourself. Remember, you have a common passion with this person – business.

> ❝Most top people are nice. They have to be, to get people to work for them.❞

Don't expect Paul House, CEO of Tim Hortons to pick up the phone when you call, of course. Top people surround themselves with 'firewalls', people trained to filter out timewasters.

Your first job is to persuade this firewall that you are not a time-waster. This is not as hard as it may sound. And remember that the firewall is not just there to get rid of wasters but to facilitate welcome callers.

Begin by finding out who Paul House's Personal Assistant (PA) or Executive Secretary is. Then send the PA a simple e-mail, explaining who you are, that you want five minutes of *their* (not their boss') time and ask them to suggest a time that would be convenient for you to call. If you get no reply, call them and leave a voicemail to this effect.

When you do speak to the Personal Assistant, say that you want to speak to Mr. House because you believe you have a business idea that would interest him. Tell them what the idea is (the premise of your elevator pitch). Add that you have the nucleus of the right team to make it work (the equivalent of the elevator pitch's endorsement). Explain why you chose Mr. House (recommendation of an instructor at the university who believed Mr. House could really provide valuable advice to this start up ...). Don't bullshit here. It'll show, and you will look ridiculous. If you are sincere, that will shine through too.

A good PA will either set up a brief conversation or say no and explain why. It may be that you have not expressed yourself quite clearly enough, which gives you the opportunity to restate your pitch. Or maybe Mr. House is not interested in mentoring, in which case thank the PA politely – and ask if they know of anyone in their organization who would be interested.

If the PA is rude, that's a sign that their boss is not right for you. The kind of people who make good mentors employ polite, intelligent PAs, not human Rottweilers.

> "A mentor is worth their weight in gold. They can be the difference between an idea's success and failure."

If the idea of making these calls still fills you with horror – were you really honest when you looked at the profile of the entrepreneur and said 'That's me'? True entrepreneurs would enjoy this process. Or they would be so passionate about their idea that they wouldn't give these sort of worries a second thought. Maybe you are better suited to be a cornerstone? Or, if you really do feel that, despite this evidence to the contrary, you are an entrepreneur by nature, then you must find a sales cornerstone who has what it takes to make these tough, 'cold' calls.

Incidentally, although the entrepreneur needs chutzpah, this shouldn't be taken too far. In the 1980s movie film *Wall Street*, Charlie Sheen's character hounds Gordon Gekko mercilessly till the big guy takes him on. This is very Hollywood, and most Canadian business people would be alienated by this. Most real, non-celluloid Americans would, too.

⇒ *'Can't we just skip this stage and get on with it?'*

No. A mentor is worth their weight in gold. They can be the difference between an idea's success and failure.

Remember that the qualities you will use and develop in the search for your mentor – courage, single-mindedness, sincerity – will be of enormous use in business later on, in dealing with colleagues and with the most important people in the universe, customers.

So go off and buy another round of drinks. Let the doubters have their say, then get on with finding a mentor.

No excuses.

What qualities must a mentor have?

Experience – the more the better. Forty years? Perfect. If you're in high technology, don't be a technosnob. The world doesn't divide into dudes or dinosaurs.

By the way … Mentorship should not be the exclusive activity of the entrepreneurial firm. A seriously-managed mentorship program is an investment every organization should consider.

The mentor must *get your idea*. In a perfect world, they would react to it with the same excitement as the entrepreneur's mates did in the pub. But they're older and wiser, so they will be much more considered. If they like you and the idea, they'll go away and assess the assumptions and logic behind it.

If they don't like the idea, don't trash it at once. Try several other people. And never settle with someone big who 'quite likes' the idea. As every sales person knows, 'maybe' is the worst possible answer. A clear 'no' sets you free to look elsewhere; an enthusiastic 'yes' means you're in business. 'Close' properly with your mentor: you are going to ask a lot of them, and they will only deliver if their belief is real.

They must like you. How do you know? You just have to use your intuition here. You have a lot to offer them in terms of enthusiasm and liveliness, so offer it, and watch them respond. Remember that they won't see you as rivals; they've been there and done it, anyway.

You must like them. As above, trust your intuition. A simple question to ask is whether you would enjoy going to the pub with this person for a couple of pints to chat about non-business related affairs?

Intuition doesn't get a lot of space in business literature, maybe because it's impossible to draw overcomplicated diagrams of it, complete with triangles, cut-away cylinders, more arrows than Custer's last stand and the word 'synergy' somewhere. But intuition is hugely valuable, especially in dealing with people. Its lack of definability makes it hard to measure, or to improve once you have made an assessment of it. The fact is that your subconscious mind is a very powerful processor-drawing far more insightful and accurate conclusions than sitting at a desk and working through a problem. When given time, the brain will often generate answers to problems that leave you wondering ... how did I come up with that? And yet ... there it is. In my opinion intuition is quite often the outcome of your collective thoughts and experiences. My experience of intuition is that almost everybody has it to a very high degree, and that the people who make bad judgements are the ones who override it in some way. If you make a run of bad judgements, ask yourself what you are putting in the way of your natural talent for spotting fakes and phonies.

Note that business has already ceased to be about spreadsheets and software, and has entered the world of personal judgement and emotions. Is this world 'easy'? As I said above, you have intuition. Trust it.

"Business has already ceased to be about spreadsheets and software, and has entered the world of personal judgement and emotions."

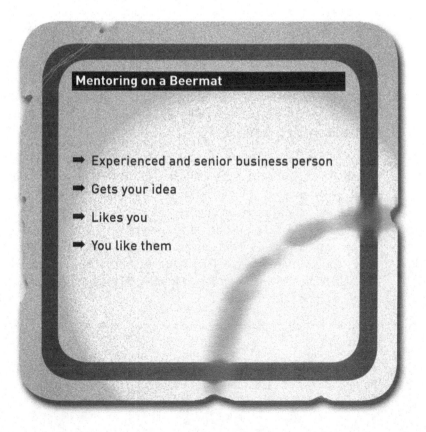

Mentoring on a Beermat

➡ Experienced and senior business person

➡ Gets your idea

➡ Likes you

➡ You like them

What does a mentor offer?

At the most basic, a mentor offers *good advice*. They will have seen similar ideas before and will have an understanding about practical difficulties, and (most important) how to get round these difficulties. They will have a broad view of the business marketplace, and will understand where the idea fits in. They may know who is most likely to be receptive to your idea as a customer – not just which company but which person in that company.

They may even know that person – and if so, this is where the mentor really earns your undying gratitude: *connections*. Anyone starting a business is depressingly familiar with interviews with well-meaning but powerless individuals from big organizations. Your enthusiastic presentation and their apparent fascination leads to 'I'll pass it on to Ms X' or 'I'll mention it at the next Z committee', after which nothing happens. Your mentor will send you direct to Ms X or to the chair of the Z committee *with a personal endorsement*. This should get you 15 minutes of that person's attention. Make sure you have a clear, concise, enthusiastic and appropriate 'pitch' ready for this. (I say 'appropriate', because you must have done your homework about *their* business before you meet them.)

Your mentor's connections are also essential if you need to raise *capital*. The mentor may invest themselves, or tell personal, and wealthy, friends. Or they can put you in touch with business angels and other potential investors. Perhaps that is the most valuable asset I have to share with my students who aspire to become entrepreneurs. My contact list is extensive and all seem ready and willing to assist. They trust me not to send someone who isn't ready or inappropriate. My role as a mentor is to challenge, support, ask, and connect.

Mentors are also invaluable in helping you find sources of *specialist advice*.

Finally, you now have the endorsement for your elevator pitch. Somebody serious is taking you seriously.

You have leapt another hurdle on your way to success.

Why do people become mentors? Basically, because they enjoy it. Obviously it's not every successful business person's flute of Bollinger, and you will spot non-mentors very quickly, as they really do not want to be bothered by 'wannabes'. But to many people it is the ideal Indian summer of their career. As a mentor you can take part in a new business venture, without having the total – and exhausting, and risky – involvement of the team at the very core.

It's also rewarding at a deeper level. Mentors have a strong desire to pass on the lessons they have learnt to the next generation – especially to people in whom they see at least partial reflections of themselves.

It beats retirement, too. Many mentors get home from their last day at HQ with the cut glass and the retirement cheque, eager to get the roses sorted out and some fishing in. Two weeks later they are bored stiff.

There is also a financial inducement – the mentor should be rewarded with a paid, non-exec position in the organization. But this is not a major motive for a mentor, who should be well enough off anyway. If you suspect that money is their main motive, you have got the wrong person. Keep looking.

Finding a mentor is not easy, but it is worth every moment you put into the search many times over.

Some lucky people do find it easy, and can have the opposite problem, that they have too many people wanting to mentor them. I used to think that you had to whittle this down to one person, but, on reflection, you can be more subtle about this. Have a special mentor for your most personal and pressing issues, but why not have a team of specialist mentors who are advisers on specific areas? Particularly special is a customer mentor – a valuable friend indeed.

Your first customer

The final item on your Original Beermat is your first customer. For the moment, enter the name in pencil. You can only use pen when they, or someone else, writes you a cheque.

The journey to that point can be a long one, but it is a real adventure. You will have the satisfaction of seeing your idea mature as you undertake it. The truth is that, however good an idea is, it won't fit into the marketplace as neatly as you think. It's only by getting close to potential customers, by hearing precisely what they need, what they can afford and how they intend to purchase it, that you can really refine a business idea and cross its fifth hurdle – that first cheque.

This is your next big challenge after finding your mentor. Listening skills are essential here – but also a measure of scepticism: comments not backed up by action are of limited value. Don't be knocked off course by well-meaning input from people who don't understand your idea or your market deeply enough. The sales cornerstone really comes into their own here, as they will naturally drive any potential customer to a 'close' – i.e. a clear 'yes' with money attached, or a firm 'no', with clear reasons why.

66The truth is that, however good an idea is, it won't fit into the marketplace as neatly as you think.99

Sending technical people into this kind of discussion can lead to fascinating debates about possible directions in widget design in 2020, but no clear commercial direction for your product, here, now. Leave the tech chat for conferences, and get the sales cornerstone earning their stake!

Remember that the ultimate judge of any commercial offering, from a corner shop to the whizziest Internet application, is the *marketplace* – not some clever analyst's report or a den full of dragons.

Seedling selling

Your mentor can often create golden sales leads for you, via a word in the ear of someone senior at an ideal target company. Use and cherish these leads.

At the same time, think of other people who would benefit from your idea, and get selling to them. Remember that word *benefit*: You're selling *benefits to the customer*, not all those wonderful *features* that your technical team spent so long building into the product. I know you've read this before, probably in every book on selling you've ever seen, but people still seem to miss this point. Acres of rainforest still disappear every year just to provide pointless corporate puffery that has only one possible response: 'So what?'

When selling to other businesses – which is what you should be doing (see pages 81–3 for a discussion on this) – the most attractive benefit is 'This will save you money'. Ideally this will be because your product does something new. Competition on pure price – 'Our widget is just like everyone else's, but cheaper' – is the worst kind of competition. Is it cheaper because it's poor quality? And for how long will you be the cheapest in the market? Quality of delivery, all the way from a cast-iron warranty to a smile on the face of the engineer, becomes a competitive factor once you are up and running, and once customers can judge the delivery for themselves. (But start off on the right foot anyway; be nice to deal with from day one.)

'Lifestyle' competition, on which many consumer markets thrive, is by far the hardest to make work, hence the huge marketing budgets thrown at it by giant multinationals. 'Our widgets are cooler!' 'Says who?'

Overleaf is a Beermat 'hierarchy of benefits'.

Rule one of selling is to understand your customers' needs. Rule two is to know your product and its benefits inside out. You begin to sell once you match your customers' needs with your product's benefits.

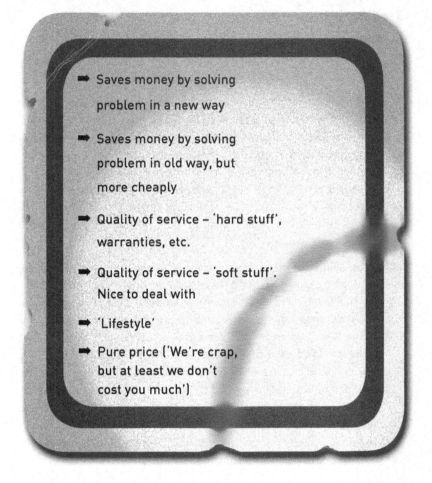

- Saves money by solving problem in a new way

- Saves money by solving problem in old way, but more cheaply

- Quality of service – 'hard stuff', warranties, etc.

- Quality of service – 'soft stuff'. Nice to deal with

- 'Lifestyle'

- Pure price ('We're crap, but at least we don't cost you much')

Time to go and pitch

People buy from people. Brochures, websites and so on are never a substitute for human contact. This is why your mentor's endorsement, and their phone call to the boss of a potential client, is so valuable. But if this is not available, how do you find the right person to speak to?

It's a bit like contacting your mentor. Get e-mailing and calling. If you are unendorsed, you won't speak to the President of the company straight off, but *someone* will answer the phone or reply to the e-mail. Get into a dialogue with them about your product and its benefits, and ask for their help. 'Who should I be speaking to?' 'What's the best way to contact them?' Phone-answerers can be extraordinarily helpful.

When you get to talk to the person you should be talking to, introduce yourself, use your elevator pitch and ask for a brief meeting. Fifteen minutes, that's all you want.

When you secure this *initial* meeting, your pitch will be longer, of course – but still keep it simple. Three big benefits maximum: one big benefit will do. The content should vary from audience to audience: it is a description of how your product will benefit *them*, not why your product is wonderful in the general scheme of things.

When making your pitch, don't feel that the longer you talk to people the more interested they are. This isn't true. Customers often become detached or loose interest in meetings, and sit listening to people they've decided not to buy from, out of a mixture of politeness, laziness (it's easier than working) and an ever-diminishing hope that you might suddenly say something that actually does interest them.

You should go into every meeting you ever have with a clear objective. Here, an order is the ideal; but more likely it will be something else useful like agreement to a trial or a further meeting – a sign that you've passed their initial 'sanity check'.

At the *next* meeting, you are definitely after an order. If you've got this far, the customer should have a real need for what you have to offer. Watch out for team meetings where everyone is keen to talk theory and technicalities and not about specifically how your product is going to be of use to them: you may be being pumped for information. But most such meetings, if set up properly and *led by your sales cornerstone*, should lead to a real outcome, either a 'yes' or a 'no' with unambiguous reasons.

Much seedling selling is like consultancy. Consultancy can be a dirty word in business circles, conjuring up preppy MBAs telling people twice their age things they know already and charging them a fortune. But the good consultant listens very carefully to what they are told, interprets that in the light of their knowledge and delivers a judgment that has real value.

You should be doing the same. You don't have a proven product to sell, but by listening carefully and thinking deeply about the client's real needs and how your offer can meet those needs, you can make a sale.

Ideally, you sell to the client so well that they agree to pay at least part of the price in advance. This is an outcome really worth striving for.

When your first customer writes out your first cheque, it's a very special moment indeed. Savour it. Once the cheque is cleared, retrieve it, frame it and hang it on your wall.

So there you have your Original Beermat: elevator pitch, mentor, first customer. Frame that, too, and hang it next to that first cheque.

You've fulfilled your Beermat Plan.

The team

The ideal team for a seedling enterprise is the entrepreneur, four cornerstones and the mentor. The mentor isn't a part of the day-to-day team, however: so on this, most basic level, the business is run by a team of *five individuals*.

Five is a magic number. Look at the great names of rock'n'roll. Boyzone, Westlife … Seriously: Oasis, The Rolling Stones, The Beatles if you include the essential contributions of Brian Epstein and then Sir George Martin.

"Five is a magic number."

There is, I believe, a reason for this. Two people are a marriage. Three people are a marriage plus an outsider. Four people are two marriages. This may sound silly, but groups of four so often split into two feuding individuals watched by two passive ones (e.g. The Beatles once they had cut themselves adrift from Sir George). Five just seems to be the number that works. It's big enough for flexibility, for grouping and regrouping of individuals round different ideas at different times. It's too small for cliques to form within it. And it's odd, so a majority vote can always be taken.

Remember that the cornerstones are not full-time from day one. What about the entrepreneur? They will really only be happy when working on the idea – but even here, I advise keeping some form of other income, even if it's only part-time, for as long as possible. However, I sympathize with anyone who jacks in a job to get really stuck into the fulfillment of their entrepreneurial dream. Like lovers who elope, it's not hugely sensible, but that's not really the point.

What should the five-person team look like? My ideal line-up is:

- The *entrepreneur*. The person with the vision and the charisma. The boss.
- The *technical innovator*. The brains behind the product. 'Supernerd', the future technical director or chief technical officer.
- The *delivery* specialist. Also a technician, but in the very different area of 'delivery'. The future operations director or chief operating officer.
- The *sales* specialist. No revenue, no business!
- The *financier*. Not expert at flashy high finance, but at cash management, cost control and managing relationships with capital providers and other professionals.

Note: the entrepreneur will probably come from a sales or technical background. They still need all four cornerstones in their start-up team, however. This is very important.

The entrepreneur's job is to keep the flame of the business' vision ablaze, both internally and when presenting the company to outsiders: to the media and to potential customers. They will probably still initiate some sales or do bits of technical work, but they must pass the core responsibility for the area where they once reigned supreme over to the more reliable cornerstones. This isn't easy, but must be done.

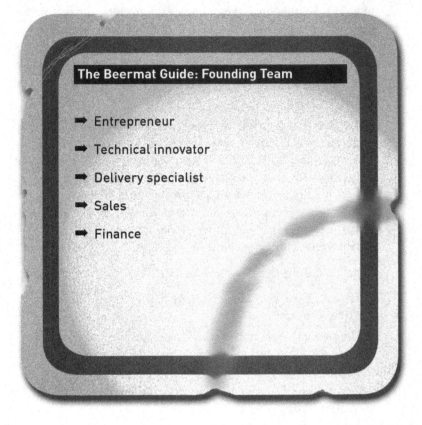

The Beermat Guide: Founding Team

➡ Entrepreneur

➡ Technical innovator

➡ Delivery specialist

➡ Sales

➡ Finance

There's another helpful little acronym. All you need is ETDSF!

Note that there are *two* technical cornerstones. This applies to most businesses I can think of. In a software house, the innovators are writing early versions of the idea, up to 1.0. This version breaks all the rules, solving pressing problems in an amazing and new way, but probably doesn't actually work. The delivery specialist then takes over, improving piecemeal – Versions 1.1, 1.2, 1.3, etc. – until a saleable product is created. While the deliverer is doing this, the innovator starts pulling the whole thing to bits and radically rethinking it to create Version 2.0, which will do more wonderful things but keeps falling over.

In a manufacturing business, the innovator's skill is about design, function, construction, materials application; the delivery specialist concentrates on processes, machinery, manning, cost efficiency, materials handling.

Innovation cornerstones ignore resource constraints: for them, anything goes, as long as it creates the new, ground-breaking product. The deliverer has to accept all existing constraints, and get the job done within those confines. Yes, this can lead to tension, but it is a useful and creative one, not just 'another spat'.

Lower-tech businesses may not need an innovator full-time – the entrepreneur will be thinking of new ways of doing what you do, and that will be enough. You could then muddle through with four cornerstones, but I much prefer odd numbers. For most enterprises there is a critical, and often rather recondite, area of expertise, mastery of which can give you a real edge. For a retail business, for example, the input of someone who is an expert on location is of immense value. Such a 'critical factor cornerstone' works alongside the delivery cornerstone (who is in charge of everything else).

Who should be in charge of basic admin? It can be the delivery cornerstone, but I think the best person for the job is the finance cornerstone. They will have a natural feel for value for money. The worst person is definitely the entrepreneur – if you let them loose in this area, it is only a matter of time before you come into the office one morning to find gold taps in the washroom, specially imported papyrus notepaper and amazing new telephones with video screens that don't quite work at the moment but the bloke who invented them is coming in next week to fix them. And no milk in the fridge.

Cornerstone stakes

Your cornerstones should have substantial stakes in the company. Not just nominal ones, but serious pieces of equity. In The Instruction Set, we split the equity five ways, and I actually think this is the best way to do things. Business is a team game. and if your team is anything less than passionate, you won't win. A 20 per cent stake gets the right people, and gives them the right motivation – which isn't just financial, but about belonging.

Entrepreneurs fear they will lose control if this five-way split is instituted. While that is technically true, a structure will soon emerge for day-to-day running of the business, with the entrepreneur at the top and the four cornerstones reporting to them. The entrepreneur is still effectively the boss – and every company must have a boss, there is no way around this. But with equal shareholdings for all, the boss has to listen very hard to the clever and passionate specialists around them, and this is exactly how it should be.

When the company gets bigger, the entrepreneur and the cornerstones (plus non-execs) will be the board. This board *must* be strong, and the only way to build strength into it is to empower its members.

"The board *must* be strong, and the only way to build strength into it is to empower its members."

I have seen so many companies where one individual, usually the entrepreneur, owns almost all the stock. And I've seen so many of them fail: the owner gets a crazy new idea, or simply refuses to listen to warnings ... Majority owners always have a gun to point at their team members: in the last resort, they can sack everybody or sell the business. And entrepreneurs aren't the most level-headed of people.

OK, in practice, few companies actually end up structured in the pure Beermat way. Few start the way we did, with five of us with strong and complementary skills and a high level of trust based on pre-existing friendships. Lone entrepreneurs or entrepreneur-plus-'foil' teams find it hard to give away huge chunks of their business to late incomers whom they don't really know that well. But I still believe that our model is the ideal one, and that in so far as a business deviates from it, it weakens itself as a whole, as a force for truly uniting the skills, commitment and passions of its key people.

Wanted: four cornerstones

How do you find these key 'right people'? There should be a nucleus of you – two or three – to start off with. The entrepreneur's magnetism will have attracted a group of individuals with, hopefully, a range of business skills.

Supposing this isn't the case? Supposing you're an entrepreneur plus a techie 'foil' only? Conventional wisdom says 'hire in accountants or sales people'. But you hardly ever get the right kind of people – proper cornerstones, with their unique mixture of solidity, entrepreneurial flair and loyalty to the business – that way.

A group of techies without an entrepreneur is in an even worse position. You will not get your business off the ground. If a group of you have a good idea, but lack the fire and charisma (and selfishness!) of the entrepreneur, find such a person *that you can trust*. Someone with a sales background would be ideal: sales people need great ideas to sell, like fish need water. (Note: don't be fooled by stereotypes of people in loud clothes on used car lots. Proper sales people are not loud and aggressive, but likeable, confident and good listeners.)

The best place to look for cornerstones is among the people you know.

A long time ago I was told that over 70% of new venture hires are acquired through personal contact and networking referrals. Simple observation and agreement from entrepreneurs would confirm this number ... and for good reason. When asked most people are pleased to recommend someone who may represent a good fit. To summarize: Networking might not directly connect you to your future cornerstones but working your network contacts to see if they know someone matching a small list of skillsets may yield amazing results.

An important caveat related to hiring friends and family. A common but false assumption is that managing family members is easier than hiring a stranger. NOT TRUE! You are establishing a second and contrary relationship with this individual. The person who you love as your sister is not necessarily the person you need to be your production cornerstone. First of all, make certain they can do the job and that their goals align with yours. Unless you separate the two relationships, you will see an erosion of one of the two relationships and in my mind burning a best friend or family relationship is not worth any advantage that may come from their working in the company with you. When bringing a friend or family member into the business the best advice is to assume nothing and discuss everything. Assuming is a very dangerous word where people are concerned.

Some students arrive at my office believing that they do not have any connections or do not know who to ask for help. One example is a soon to be 'known' entrepreneur who dropped by my office one day to share his idea and solicit feedback. Frankly, I was impressed. We went on to discuss how to build his team and he confessed to not knowing anyone that could help. After thirty minutes of questioning ... he had a list of people to ask. Sometimes the entrepreneur looks at people in only one context. For example, the person you play hockey with in the recreation league may also be a highly qualified web designer. Get to know more about the people in your life – you may be surprised.

In short, your mentor may also have suggestions, but look among your personal contacts first.

"The best place to look for cornerstones is among the people you know."

Because I have been in business a long time, I now have a list of people that I know personally and whom I know would make good cornerstones. I use this list whenever I am involved in a start-up. If you do not have such a list, think about developing one. Remember that it's not a list of ideal people from 'out there', but people you know and like.

Supposing you have exhausted your contacts, and your mentor's contacts, and still have gaps? One simple answer is to wait. As an aspiring entrepreneur you will be networking anyway and you will meet the right person in time.

When the right person arrives, offer them the market rate for what they do – but a real cornerstone will be in this for adequate money, lots of fun and huge long-term potential. If the potential cornerstone asks for silly money, they are not right for the job. My recommendation for such deluded individuals is that they spend six months as a hospital porter or staff nurse, after which they might have recovered from the idea that the world automatically owes them $400,000 per annum or whatever preposterous salary they are expecting.

Don't forget that you do not have to take cornerstones on full-time to start with (yes, I know I've said this already, but it's a point many people miss, and it is essential). Accountants in particular can be 'virtual finance cornerstones' for several businesses, becoming full-time when one business gets so demanding that they have to.

How should you offer equity? It's useful to think of an original nucleus (entrepreneur plus friends in the pub) and latecomers (people recruited later to fill any skill gaps in that original group). The nucleus should split the business between themselves at once, then give full equity stakes to latecomers once latecomers have shown they have what it takes. Latecomers will want clear milestones: not always easy to offer, as the appointment of cornerstones is best done on 'feel'. There's no easy answer to this, but I make two observations. One is the importance of talking. You, the entrepreneur, should communicate well with potential cornerstones. If you don't, then the relationship is not working and they are not right for you (and vice versa!). If you do communicate, then they should be able to say, 'I've enjoyed doing this stuff, but I need a decision soon about the cornerstone stake.' You should be able to answer with equal frankness. My other observation is that you tend to know pretty early on if someone is cornerstone material.

Supposing there is disagreement in the nucleus about a latecomer? There must be unanimity in the existing founding team on any new members: the potential cornerstone has to go.

Two 'don'ts'. Don't take on a cornerstone – or anyone else, actually – because they 'look good on paper'. I wouldn't take on an assistant toilet cleaner on this kind of 'recommendation', and here we're talking about someone who will effectively be a blood brother or sister for the next five years of your life.

Don't rely on profiling systems, either. You can run some as a kind of check if you like, but don't use them for selection. Your intuition is a much sharper tool.

It may be a while before you have your four cornerstones in place – the right four people, with the right skills, commitment and passion for the enterprise. When this happens, your idea will have leapt another hurdle, that of totally convincing four very able people to commit themselves to it.

The long haul

Cornerstones aren't short-termers. They're in this for the long haul. And they're prepared to give it all they've got.

Such commitment can be stressful. Set rules about things like holidays. Good companies understand the value of vacation and a full break from the rigors and demands of the company. To take a communications device or check business emails when away is, in my mind, irresponsible to yourself AND YOUR BUSINESS. It shows that the company can't function without you. This is a sign of weakness in the organization. I recall a pivotal moment in my company when I was away for five weeks. Every day I would call in to see what fires I needed to put out – after all who else could do it? After four consecutive days I was firmly (and not politely) told to stop calling. If I was needed, they would contact me. My first reaction – after concluding the call, was hurt. Then came the realization that I have an amazing team who can manage without me. I had given them the confidence, knowledge and skills to carry on. Every entrepreneur should strive to build such a team. A two week holiday should be a two week holiday and not involve any contact with the company. If it fails in your absence you suck as a leader. GET OVER YOURSELF!

Long commutes also cause stress. If you're going to be living and breathing a business for five years, move close to it. Walking or cycling distance, preferably.

All this points to the desirability of becoming an entrepreneur before you acquire a family. Of course, if you have a family, this does not disqualify you from enterprise (any more than age does: Ray Kroc founded McDonald's in his 50s). But if you are in your early 20s, unattached and eager to found a business, now is the ideal time!

Non-execs

As well as cornerstones, you can have other sources of leadership at your disposal. Your mentor should be non-executive chair of the business. And how about some other non-executive directors? These are people who don't have the intimate connection to the business that the founding five have, but who bring to it expert knowledge, and do so with the mentor's motivation of interest and involvement rather than hard cash.

As with cornerstones, recruit non-execs personally. They are part of the team, remember. When you've done so, use them well. They have expertise and influence, but can only use these if you are totally honest with them. It's no use treating them like a teacher or parent you want to hide things from (don't laugh – I've seen people do it). The more they know – warts and all – the more help they can be.

❝Go and ask their help, and it's amazing what they can do.❞

Non-execs can be of particular use if you have one specific problem that none of you five founders seem able to solve. Go and ask their help, and it's amazing what they can do.

Sadly not all non-execs fall into the above category, however. There are two types of non-exec who are worse than useless.

One is the 'letterhead non-exec'. I have seen several companies where retired celebs or members of the aristocracy are made non-exec directors, in a bid to impress people with their name on the notepaper. This is silly: nobody of any importance is impressed by this. Of course, if the celeb/aristo has amazing contacts that they really can activate, then they can earn their fee.

The other is the externally appointed non-exec. These people are placed on boards by external equity holders (usually venture capitalists). My experience of such people is that (a) they have little actual experience of running businesses, and (b) probably because they secretly know (a) but would rather die than admit it, spend board meetings quibbling about minutiae, raising irrelevant points and generally trying to show everyone how clever they are. Of course, if you've sold a chunk of your business to a VC, then you may well have to put up with this kind of bumptious show-off. So try and find other sources of finance.

So, choose non-execs whom you respect, who have contacts and experience, who bring a fresh perspective to the party, and who are nice people to work with.

How to compete

Now you are truly in business, I should say a bit about how to compete. I'm a great believer in competition – it drives innovation and stops businesses becoming smug and arrogant towards their customers. But it isn't a religion. There comes a point where competitiveness becomes destructive, both to the business and to the individuals practising it.

When you start selling your product, you will inevitably hear people say 'So it's a bit like the widgets that ABC make'. Imagine these two responses:

- *Sales person A*: 'Them! We hate those guys. Their stuff is rubbish.'
- *Sales person B*: 'Oh, yes, ABC. I've heard they're a good company and make a good product. But our product offers these special benefits ...'

It sounds obvious which is the more mature approach, but I have heard – and been horrified by – grown, adult, highly paid sales people reacting like A.

When I run a sales department, bad-mouthing the opposition is a disciplinable, and ultimately dismissible offence. Customers may well know people in the opposition, and will probably have been using their products quite happily for years. Are you telling them they're stupid? Anyway, customers are not interested in squabbles between suppliers; they are interested in getting their needs met. If you can do better than the opposition, prove it in a positive way.

Demeaning comments about the competition often has bad personal side-effects, too. People who practise it seem to become less pleasant, and less happy. One of the purposes of this book is to help readers make money and grow personally in the process: becoming twisted with loathing for your competition is not the way to a full, rich life.

When I run sales teams, I keep competition at a level where you can have a drink with the opposition and conduct a proper conversation with them. Sport played in the right spirit has the same credo. Hard, fair competition on the field; a drink in the bar afterwards.

Supposing the opposition get rough?

Sport provides a good analogy again:

Sidney Crosby was often on the receiving end of numerous penalties but he maintained focus for the task at hand, never lowering himself to their level. One of the purposes of dirty tactics is to take the victim's mind off their proper task, which in business is serving the customer.

The White Paper

You've sold your idea. Then you deliver it, and the customer is satisfied. Better, the customer is delighted. It did what you said it would, apart from a few glitches which you went in and fixed straight away, at no extra cost.

The idea has just leapt over another hurdle. It has become a proper product, and it's time to set out the nature and benefits of that product, formally.

You do this in a White Paper. This is a semi-technical document, explaining the product and its real value proposition in depth, including as much about how it is being used by your first customer as confidentiality will allow. It should be no longer than 10 sides (some people let it run to 20, but the Beermat approach is always to favour brevity). Page one should be an executive summary of the following nine, stressing the three (or fewer) main benefits the product has brought.

"The idea has just leapt over another hurdle. It has become a proper product."

If you can get your customer to write your White Paper, even better. Before sending it to potential new customers, have your mentor read through it. They will view it from a customer's perspective. I have reviewed many proposals, white papers and business plans. Often I return them and ask them to rewrite the document in their words and with meaning. There is no need to dazzle with words constantly drawn from a thesaurus or crafting a lengthy scene when one line will suffice. Stick to the point, make it succinct and meaningful. More often than not I am recommending a shorter version with more relevance. The people who will need to read your plan are busy and do not want to have a five kilogram document placed on their lap.

The White Paper has two purposes. Externally, it is to send to prospects before a first meeting, to familiarize them with your product so that at that meeting they ask the right questions –

how the product can really help them. Internally, it concentrates the team on where the product has got to, which may now be something very different from your good-enough idea in the pub.

Beyond the first sale

Your first sale was a great moment: you were right to celebrate it. But don't get carried away and start ramping up borrowing and spending. You must now start building a portfolio of customers. The aim should be to have 10 or 15 regular customers, none of whom is responsible for more than 15 per cent of your income, plus a back-up list of 20 potential customers that you are researching and getting to know. As this begins to come about, your business starts to change. You need to start taking people on. Planning becomes more complicated and more important.

You are growing into a sapling enterprise.

Sometimes, sadly, you make one sale, get your White Paper all written up, then all goes quiet. Despite all your best efforts, you've made one sale and no more ... It's unusual, but it can happen.

You need to ask yourself what the market really is for your product. Maybe there is only one buyer. If so, you must diversify – what else can you do with the skills that developed that product so successfully? (It is a success, as someone has bought it.) Can you sell more things to your one, satisfied customer? (Not an ideal situation, as it keeps you in their power, but better than no business at all.) If neither of these options seems to work, then it might be necessary to pull the plug. Don't give up easily, but if you really have tried all possible avenues and still only made a single, one-off sale, then don't be ashamed to get working on something new.

However, *by far* the most likely outcome is that further sales will follow. Start thinking in terms of that portfolio of actual and potential customers ...

Early pricing

Pricing something new is hard. Just how much is it worth? It's always worth looking round the market at products most like yours. Be humble: few products are actually as radical as the originators believe them to be. What is your nearest rival, and what do they charge?

But that's only a guideline. What *really* matters in pricing is how much the product is worth to the customer, which is closely related to how much money it will save or make them (assuming they are business customers: see the discussion on page 81–2). So the more you know about your customer's business – not just roughly what they make and do, but the precise details of how they do it and at what cost – the better placed you are to guess the right price for your product. Your sales cornerstone should be talking to your main potential customers in depth anyway: listen to them.

Don't be in a hurry to issue a formal price list. You are not yet delivering standard products. Delivery will still involve a lot of customization, and even outright invention, this early in a business.

"Be humble: few products are actually as radical as the originators believe them to be."

If you are fully funded, you can offer early adopters low prices, on the clear understanding that the prices will rise as they use your product more and more. Don't try and fool people into buying cheap then turning round and stinging them with a price hike: let them know in advance of your pricing plans. If they like your product and it clearly makes or saves them money, they will be happy to pay a fair rate.

Remember that while nobody likes to pay more for something than they have to, the ultimate aim of all negotiation is 'win-win' situations, where each party gains.

The Real Business Plan

We're now all painfully familiar with those fantasy business plans for products that have not yet made any sales. You know the scenario: 'The world market in shoes is $220 billion, and we aim to get a 1 per cent share of this. No, we haven't actually sold a single pair yet ...'

But once you have started making real sales to real customers, then you have a real business, and that needs a Real Business Plan. You have an idea of what your market is and who your actual rivals are going to be. You have one actual and several potential customers, and should have some idea of how much they are likely to buy and when. You need to plan your recruitment strategy, your cash flow ...

Like the White Paper, the Real Business Plan has internal and external value. Internally (its biggest benefit), it focuses the team. Externally, it will be of use if you find yourself in need of development capital – but see the section 'Seedling funding', on page 41: people get real benefit from what you produce, so try and get them to pay up front for it!

The contents of the Real Business Plan are outlined below.

When you draw up this plan, don't be afraid to get help. MBA students are ideal for this sort of thing. Find one who isn't appallingly arrogant – they do exist, I promise – and get them to help you draw up the plan. Employ a market specialist to make market assessments sound (and be) convincing. You should have a financial cornerstone in place by now, but if you haven't, get a bright business school student to help you draw up the spreadsheets.

Note that if the MBA or the student click with you and the team, they may come and join you. In the sapling stage, bright, young team members are what you need.

Some of the terms in the Plan are self-explanatory (or have already been explained). To comment on others ...

The Real Business Plan

1. Elevator pitch
2. Mission statement
3. Tactical sales plan. Your next 10 customers, and what you intend to sell them, in what time frame
4. Any strategic alliances you intend to form, in order to expedite these sales or their delivery
5. Delivery plan. How these 10 sales will be delivered
6. People plan. The most important part of the whole plan. Who is going to do what? If you need to hire new people in, what sort of people and when? How will everyone's delivery against the people plan be measured?
7. Financial projections

Mission statement

It's easy to be cynical about these, but if they are sincere and specific, they are of great value. Missions are about purpose. What is the purpose of this company? Not just 'to make money'. Entrepreneurs aim to change the way things are done. The company mission is to effect that change. What are you going to change and how? Go into a little more detail than the elevator pitch – but not too much.

The mission statement should also outline any other things you plan to do different in matters such as staff motivation, design (or whatever operational areas in which you plan to innovate).

Mission statements also capture the personality of the firm as expressed in the values. This can often help distinguish the business and make it unique. One of the most satisfying aspects of entrepreneurship is that these values are an extension of what is important to you. You are able to express your values through your company and, in so doing; you should be making your firm unique and interesting. Remember two important questions: 'What is our company going to look like to the world out there?' and 'What will it be like to work in?' The last question is hugely important, and the answer should be 'fun'. The dour old Dickensian image of work is history. The best people are motivated by enthusiasm, passion, purpose – by a mission.

"The best people are motivated by enthusiasm, passion, purpose – by a mission."

Strategic alliances

This might seem a rather pompous term to have in so youthful a document as your Real Business Plan (the company is still only a few sales old!). But it is never too early to start thinking about these. Who could you help sell more of their product? No matter how big they are, if you think you can help, then talk to them. Get them to trial one of their machines featuring your widget, or to have a section in their shop selling your ethically made clothes.

Although the sales cornerstone may have views on this, it is the entrepreneur who is most likely to suggest alliances. It is certainly part of the entrepreneur's job to set up such alliances. Partially because of that perpetually useful charisma; partially because as CEO they can approach senior people in big companies on a 'level footing'; partially because, when all's said and done, they remain the overall expert on the business, its markets and direction.

For a small company that believes it can be a real strategic partner to a big one, an excellent place to approach the big fish is at trade shows, where top sales people from the big one are often manning stands and keen to talk to people. Take them off for a drink, get them talking about their customers' needs and how, maybe, you could help ... They may not 'bite', in which case you at least tried, but if your product is good and you have done your homework, then you stand a good chance of success.

In the software/high-tech industry, the best strategic partners are manufacturers, not service companies. The logo of a big service provider might look good on your website, but they can drop alliances very quickly.

The Real Business Plan is effectively a blueprint for the transition to the next stage in the company's life. Once you start making those planned next 10 sales, you will need to start taking people on to deliver against them, and the glory days of the five of you against the world will be over. Shame, in a way – business may never be quite as much fun. But you have no option but to move on, so do so joyfully. Onwards and upwards!

Before moving to the next stage, however, there are plenty of issues still to be discussed about life in the seedling stage. Most important of all is probably ...

Finance

This book is a general guide, and there is not room to go into depth on this essential subject. Anyone and everyone starting a business *must* investigate this topic further.

Along with this, the finance cornerstone should be chief cost-controller of the business. Everyone else will want to spend money on their area; the finance cornerstone must keep this within what is feasible. Even sales people's expenses!

Naturally, the finance cornerstone is in charge of funding.

Before you open the doors on day one, you need to understand what your cashflow requirements will be. I know this is a difficult (and sometimes painful) exercise, but not having sufficient seed money or start-up capital will start you off in a deficit position and it will be extremely difficult to climb your way out of that hole. Ensure you secure the required initial capital and not a penny less before your first day in business. You need to be focused on growing your business. Dodging creditors because you are underfunded takes up precious time and energy.

1. In the early stages it is all about the cash flow. You need to understand what is coming in and going out every day. This will help you understand where the money is going and when; when new money is needed and how much;

2. Understand the value of opportunity cost. While an economic expression, it has a powerful impact on decision making where money is concerned I don't understand this one).

3. Build proper, effective, disciplined financial tracking systems immediately. Shoe box financials do not work. The low cost of decent accounting systems will yield immediate benefit. Setting the financial disciplines early in your business career will ensure that not only you, but the people you employ long term will follow those disciplines without fail. Make sure you adhere to all government regulations.

4. Always require two signatures on each cheque (the entrepreneur and the finance cornerstone).

5. Match your type of loan to the purpose (short term need with short term loan). Be prepared and willing to negotiate.

6. Your bank account manager should be kept abreast of activity. Provide accurate and timely reports. It doesn't have to be a painful experience.

I am going to draw on an individual with whom I remain a huge fan – my brother Mike. When my father decided to leave our family business to accept a role in a large firm that offered a healthy pension plan (something often not found in small businesses), Mike quickly and very capably took his place as my partner. At eighteen he possessed three of the most critical attributes to success: a tenacious work ethic; a hunger to learn; and a balance between conventional wisdom and disruptive thinking. After I left the firm he showed his true colours and brilliance by building several very successful companies. I've taken the liberty of integrating Mike's comments with some of the original suggestions provided in the Beermat.

As the entrepreneur, you always should see and sign every cheque that is cut, however with automation becoming more prevalent, many transactions take place on a daily basis that do not involve a cheque. With electronic fund transfers and wire payments, you must ensure there is a process in place that accounts for how these types of payments are handled. Even if you are the one making the payments in the early years, ensure there is a process in place that is repeatable. There are two basic reasons for establishing this protocol: (a) there is good control, and (b) you actually see what your hard-earned cash is being spent on.

Always borrow on long-term if you can; an overdraft can be called in at any time whereas a lease or a three-year term loan gives you certainty of cash flow. As your business grows and develops, your financing needs will as well. In the early years, you may have to finance certain items that will someday be a cash purchase. As long as you are aware of the borrowing cost, pay special consideration to alternative ways of paying for products and services in the early years.

Do a regular cash flow forecast and always take the most conservative approach to cash flow.

Try to persuade suppliers to give you extra payment terms – 60 rather than 30 days to pay. If you are in a weak position and can not pay suppliers as agreed, never hide from them or avoid payment. Instead, contact them, be honest about your situation and ask them for help. A good supplier will always work with a growing business as they see the long term opportunity.

Don't avoid paying the necessary taxes. Always remember that it is not your money when you consider withholding taxes and source deductions. You are holding these funds in trust. Never count those funds in your cash flow as it is not your money to spend. The penalties associated with late payment of withholding taxes or source deductions are crippling so NEVER get in a position where you can not afford to make those payments.

Get your financial control systems and documentation processes right from day one. Too many people simply start, then worry about the audit trail or evidence for expenses afterwards. This inevitably leads to problems. Set up simple automated systems – record all invoices, all expenses requiring receipts, time reporting – on day one. There are simple and inexpensive accounting systems easily obtainable for use with your personal computer. Better yet, hire a part time bookkeeper to ensure your finances are kept in order. This will allow you to focus on your core responsibility which is growing your business. Any time spent that is not directly related to growing your business is wasted time.

Cashflow needs to be considered with every decision you make. Don't spend money that you don't have, in the vain hope that money will be found somewhere. This is the quickest route to bankruptcy. If you haven't actually got the cash today, don't spend it. As well, while monitoring cash, always remember, your available cashflow is NOT what you have in the bank, however it is the difference between what you have in the bank and what your commitments for the next 30 days are.

When making commitments to your suppliers, it is important that you keep your credit rating in mind. Your credit rating determines whether suppliers will give you credit or demand cash, so invest the time and research your own credit on a regular basis. Any irregularities can be reported and changed.

Whether you are borrowing or not, keep the bank well-informed and up-to-date on progress. Although this may seem obvious, it is important to be honest with your banker. Whether you have good or bad news to report, always ensure you provide them with accurate and timely information so that, if you want to borrow to expand, they know you and your business and they trust you. Your banker can be your greatest ally or your worst enemy. You create that relationship.

In summary I learned one very important rule early in my business career. That simple rule is "Cash is King"! With every decision you make, you need to think about the repercussions from a cashflow perspective in order to survive.

"If you haven't actually got the cash today, don't spend it."

Seedling funding

Some companies work very hard to avoid any outside financing. I recommend you move heaven and earth to do the same, partly because external funding is a nightmare, but mainly because refusing to rely on it imposes a financial and sales discipline on the business that is very, very healthy.

High-tech companies will find it hard to follow this route, as they need substantial upfront capital for prototype development and early manufacturing. Biotech enterprises, for example: you'll hardly be able to develop a world-beating cancer drug on early revenue plus a few hundred thousand from a friend of the mentor. But if they take a Beermat approach, they will look at all possible ways of funding from revenue before getting substantial external funding. Can they, for example, set up some kind of services arm to fund the development of the core project? I've met a biotech company doing exactly that: there are two businesses, one of which provides assistance with drug trials and yields cash, while the other spends the cash developing products.

If you really do have no option but to fund externally, two golden rules apply. The first is to get someone very tough on your side. The average entrepreneur is convinced they are the toughest negotiator in town – but the average professional investor will eat them for breakfast. Your mentor may well be the right person to help here, or a top-class law firm (the best ones do good deals for entrepreneurs, hoping to grow their revenue from you as your business grows).

The second rule is to be choosy. It's not about the best terms, but the right people. You're inviting external funders into your business: make sure that they bring more than money; make sure they bring real skills and contacts.

Here is my Beermat list of funding sources, in descending order of desirability.

First and best is your own money. Simple as that.

An alternative is family money. There are success stories about businesses founded with family money – but an awful lot of 'family money' ventures seem to fail. There may be obscure Freudian reasons behind this, but I think it is more likely just 'easy come, easy go'. Unless you have had to sweat for the money, you'll bottle out of those tough financial decisions at the margin that can make the difference between success and failure. If you are going to approach family and friends for money PLEASE apply the following principles:

1. Treat them as investors and not as family and friends. This will force you to behave in a different way with a more professional approach;

2. Set up a meeting with an agenda and present a copy of your business plan and/ or other documents to enhance your legitimacy. The last reason you want them to invest is because they care for you.

3. Offer specific terms. If it is debt financing, provide a repayment schedule that is fair and understood. If it is equity, clearly state what they get in return and why the proposed numbers make financial and investment sense.

4. Show your passion AND professionalism. If this sounds like a meeting with a banker or potential investor – it is!

5. Never ASSUME they know what is going on. Maintain constant contact with all investors including family and friends. Regular updates are critical even if the news isn't good.

Money borrowed from friends seems to suffer the same fate of vanishing too easily. The friendship usually vanishes with it BUT doesn't have to be this way.

Second, for those of us who don't have private money, there may be grants or loans available from institutions like the Canadian Youth Business Foundation. The CYBF is an excellent organization, which really does want to help young people with bright ideas. One of their most impressive support mechanisms is through their mentorship program.

The Government-funded Regional Development Agencies also run various schemes – contact your local Small Business Centre or your municipal Economic Development Office (the address will be in the phone book, or go online) to find out which ones are available in your area. Your bank should know about schemes like the Small Firms Loan Guarantee – though sometimes they need a little prodding to open up about this.

Government assistance can involve form-filling: a job for the finance cornerstone, not the impatient entrepreneur.

Third, revenue. If you have a product that sounds capable of making a real difference to your customers' business, ask for payment in advance. Your customer may need reassurance on quality and delivery. Provide it. You want to be the best anyway. They may ask for a discount for advance payment. As long as this isn't *a lot* more expensive than a bank loan, accept it.

"Your customer may need reassurance on quality and delivery. Provide it.**"**

Fourth, your mentor. If your mentor really likes you and your idea, they may well make an investment themselves. They are part of the team, and this investment cements the relationship. Note that the mentor's true motive is fun, not profit. But at the same time, it is not 'soft money', like daddy's or a friend's.

Fifth, a friend of the mentor, who is also investing for the pleasure of involvement rather than straight financial gain.

After these, there comes a big, big gap. Are you really sure none of the above avenues are open to you? Think again, as next comes ...

Sixth, bank lending. There is often a 'culture clash' between banks and entrepreneurs. Bank managers like spreadsheets, regular income flows and predictability; entrepreneurs like brainstorming sessions (led by them), big deals and the thrill of the unexpected. The solution to this clash is to have the finance cornerstone deal with the bank. They will understand what information the bank wants, and will be able to deliver it in language the bank understands. Finance cornerstones know that banks hate surprises. So they keep bank managers informed about how things are going. If you do this and things start going wrong, the bank is much more likely to be helpful.

But, as recent events have shown, banks can also change the rules. Do all you can to avoid banks taking 'charges' on your property when you start, and on your firm's assets as you grow (a loan to cover a specific asset, secured on that asset, is much healthier than more general loans which give the bank power over a range of assets).

After the banks, you have to start handing out chunks of equity to outsiders.

Seventh in my list of finance sources is a 'strategic option', where a customer agrees to pay in advance, but insists on the right to invest money in the company at a preferential rate when you next raise finance. This is the nicest form of losing equity. You get some money up front, and when the options are exercised you do lose a chunk of equity, but you have a partner on board who lives and breathes your business, rather than a financial institution that just looks at the money that comes out of the end of it. But you've still lost a chunk of your company.

There is also a freedom issue. Think this through carefully before entering into such an agreement. Will your new partner start calling the shots? Will you be able to do business with their rivals?

Despite these objections, this 'strategic stake' became a popular form of investment in the last decade, and though the options craze of that era died with dotcom mania, it is still a popular solution to funding problems.

Eighth on my list come business angels – individuals with typically up to $1 million to invest in enterprises that attract them. These fall into two categories. The first bring a huge amount to the party as well as money: they are mentors, with all those mentor benefits of experience and contacts. The best ones have fantastic market knowledge – they've probably walked the course you are just starting on. Such people are invaluable, and

I have only put them low on my list because they may well ask for a cornerstone-size chunk of equity. Fine: this kind of angel deserves it – though be wary of anyone who wants more than 25 per cent, as the locus of power in your organization must remain inside the founding team.

They are called Angels for a less obvious reason. You may meet them and not know they are angels. They do not have signs hanging on their neck proclaiming they have money and expertise to share. They only identify when inspired. Some form groups which can be identified and pursued but many more choose not to be exposed.

Much less attractive are what I call fallen angels – investors who don't offer much mentoring but are just in it for the money. Like VCs (see below), these people are a last resort. Try to find a mentor/investor, for whom the title 'angel' is not ironic.

Your mentor should be able to suggest angels. If not, look around for your local angel networks (angels prefer to invest locally). At the same time, keep asking around about other local networks that might operate more informally.

Ninth, venture capitalists (VCs). Most start-ups shouldn't go within 100 miles of these people. They are *strictly* only for businesses that have enormous start-up costs and no way of bringing in any revenue till late in the development process.

If you do fall into that tiny category of businesses that can only be funded by VCs, please be very careful in your dealings with these people. They are very ruthless. Get someone equally ruthless on your side.

VCs can play games like stringing out negotiations (so the cash-hungry entrepreneur gets ever more desperate) and changing terms at the last minute. They will insist on fearsome clauses in deals that virtually wipe out earlier investors (anti-dilution clauses) or that ensure that if a successful exit is reached the VC gets almost all the money, even if they have not put up most of the capital (liquidation rights). They also have a reputation for promising more than they deliver in non-financial areas: they

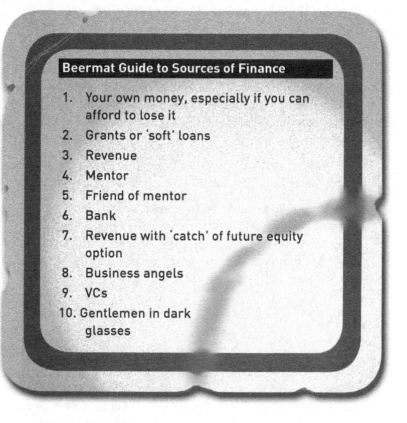

Beermat Guide to Sources of Finance

1. Your own money, especially if you can afford to lose it
2. Grants or 'soft' loans
3. Revenue
4. Mentor
5. Friend of mentor
6. Bank
7. Revenue with 'catch' of future equity option
8. Business angels
9. VCs
10. Gentlemen in dark glasses

say they'll provide help with marketing and contacts, but in my experience they lose interest once the deal is signed.

❝Get someone equally ruthless on your side.❞

VCs also impose a fast growth model on any business in which they get involved. One can hardly blame them for this, but if your plan is for anything other than hell-for-leather growth, you must find other sources of funding.

You've probably gathered I'm not a huge fan of VCs. I think they are far too interested in money and far too uninterested in what business is really about: people, change, customers. I accept that in certain cases they have helped businesses grow, but most of the entrepreneurs I know hate them. I wish this were not the case, but that's how it is.

Never mind; as I've said, the overwhelming majority of start-ups do not need to get involved with VCs, and should not. Maybe later, when your business is a 'mighty oak', but I'll talk about that later ...

Any other sources of finance? Well, there's always organized crime, but their debt collection methods are a bit draconian ...

My top tip here is 'move heaven and earth to fund from revenue and grow organically'. If you must have outsiders, do not be hypnotized by the depth of their pockets: find backers who really bring something to the party in terms of enthusiasm, expertise and solid-gold contacts.

The law

You don't need an in-house lawyer. Legal advice is best bought in for *essential legal work* such as partnership agreements, leases, warranties and employment contracts. The best lawyers have standard formulae for these: boilerplate contracts with schedules to particularize them. These should cost hundreds rather than thousands of dollars. Bad lawyers string work out; don't let them get away with this!

Lawyers who do string work out sometimes complain that they have been given such a poor brief that it's taken them all this time to understand what their clients really want. Maybe that's true sometimes – certainly don't leave yourself open to this response. Be clear with these guys.

As usual, ask your mentor for advice when selecting your lawyers. When you have chosen, get the finance cornerstone to deal with them. Financial minds are much closer to legal ones than technical, sales or entrepreneurial minds are – and the finance cornerstone will keep an eye on legal costs.

Registration

For legal and tax reasons, you should consider becoming a legal corporation from day one – certainly from that second meeting in the pub. Your business will then be called 'Inc. or Limited' and can have shareholders. In addition to debt instruments, shareholders represent a second source of capital. You can remain a corporation forever, an attractive course of action – see the comments about s,tock exchange listing later on.

It's getting easier and easier to do company registration yourself via the Internet or by visiting your local economic development office or small business support centre. If you really don't fancy doing that, ask your solicitor if they have a fixed price service whereby they will register you.

Take a little time to ponder your company name. It should be memorable; it should be appropriate to your customer group it should tell people what you do. If you really can't think of a name, have an informal chat with someone in advertising: these people often have a knack for thinking up snappy names. Or was there someone at school who always came up with catchy and probably not very flattering nicknames for people?

"Take a little time to ponder your company name. It should be memorable."

Once you have your name, of course, get your *domain* name registered as quickly as possible. Ideally, you should choose a domain name which:

- is relevant to your business
- is relatively simple – try spelling it over the phone to someone to test this
- has both .com and .ca still available (buy both, to stop rivals buying the one you don't and creating havoc).

Duties of directors

When you register a company, you become a company director. This means you are taking on certain legal responsibilities. I recommend a brief chat with your lawyer – don't be scared off by this stuff, but just be aware of it.

Patents

If you have a good idea, people will try to steal it. That's a fact of life.

The challenge with patent law is twofold. The first is that you need money to defend your patent when others attempt to encroach on your intellectual property. The second is that some organizations sit on patents waiting, like vultures, for another firm to invade their patent. This will allow them to sue and continue to enjoy the lavish lifestyle associated with vulture lawsuits. Do not get me wrong ... patent protection is important but when a firm has no intention of developing a product or service with the patent and only wish to sue those who do – well that is slimy.

The problem is that most theft of intellectual property is rather subtler than this. Once a piece of plagiarism amends an original work by quite a small amount, it ceases legally to be theft.

While I believe there is a role for patent lawyers, especially in areas like biotech, they can cost a lot of money and end up not protecting your intellectual property rights (IPR) anyway – not through incompetence but because the task is just too difficult.

The best protection of IPR is execution. Not, sadly, of copycats, but in your business: the speed and quality of your delivery. If you are genuinely the first person with an idea, you should be able to bring it to market quickest. That's your first protection: being there first. But that's only the start, as prophets of 'first mover advantage' found out. Once you are there, make sure you deliver superbly – on time; in an efficient, friendly, businesslike manner. If you do this, someone who contacts your customers saying 'We do this, too' will be sent away, even if the copycat is cheaper. People don't like changing suppliers, and only do so if forced by continuing poor delivery, ridiculously excessive prices or a step change in the market that renders the product obsolete.

Inevitably, there will come a time when there are a number of copycat products around. Don't be dragged into a price war or endless litigation: keep improving the product and its delivery.

At the same time, take obvious precautions against IPR theft by writing © on documents like course materials, registering trademarks, and patenting formulae and key designs.

If I sound vague here, it is because what is 'possible to patent' varies so much from business sector to business sector. If you have experience in the sector in which your start-up is running – and you, or some of your cornerstones, should have this experience – you will have a feel for what can and what can't realistically be protected. Be guided by this.

Finally, don't lose sleep. In business, ideas are ten-a-penny: what really matters is always delivery. Entrepreneurs often think they have 'totally original ideas' and are terrified that someone will steal them. Actually very few ideas are totally original, and if they are, they may not be good *business* ideas, as they might be too far ahead of the market. Leonardo da Vinci didn't get rich out of flying machines. But even if the idea is original and relevant, it is only the beginning of the journey to business success. Remember Edison's remark about genius being 1 per cent inspiration and 99 per cent perspiration.

Litigation

Avoid at all costs! The sad truth about litigation is that once you end up in a court, you have already lost. Only the lawyers win.

And the media, if there's a vicar or a soap star involved. If you are on the verge of litigation, stop and ask why. Then sort the problem another way.

Don't litigate, negotiate.

Legal problems almost always arise from poor communication. When you made that first deal, both parties intended to benefit from it. You would get money; your customer would get a product or service that was of use to them. So what has gone wrong? It's time to start negotiating.

Initial deals – and many subsequent deals – are often not based on formal, legally binding contracts. The acceptance is usually verbal. Once a verbal agreement has been reached, you draw up a 'memorandum of understanding' (aka a 'heads of agreement', a term which will amuse anyone with a naval background). This outlines what you intend to deliver, and how and when and to what standard, and what (and how and when) the customer intends to pay for it. Note that this memorandum also cements the relationship with the client: if a client refuses to agree to this memorandum, this is a real danger signal that they might be timewasters, simply trying to gain free market information, or that they are up to some internal political game in their own organization.

"Legal problems almost always arise from poor communication."

Once delivery begins, your sales cornerstone must monitor the process. Is the customer happy? Are things working out as planned? Keep a record of meetings and conversations, so if things do get nasty, you have a record of what occurred (though even these are of limited use in court). Remember the story of Theseus, who laid a trail of silk behind him when he went into the Minotaur's labyrinth. The Minotaur, a beast with a bull's head and a man's body and which ate nothing but human flesh, was a lot less scary than most lawyers.

The moment you begin to suspect things aren't going to plan – talk to the client. And listen to the client. Some clients 'try it on', but most don't. Maybe you're not delivering quite what they expected, or the product isn't working as well as expected, or their own needs are changing. Deal with these issues.

Note the importance of keeping the sales team involved with the customer. Businesses selling direct to consumers hand these consumers over from sales to 'customer services' the moment the sale is made. This is annoying enough if you buy baked beans, and appalling practice in a small, business-to-business organization. I am a huge believer of having a team manage the entire sales process – from research to retention. Hand-offs from one representative to another to another simply serve to alienate the customer. Look at banks with the revolving door account representative approach to clients.

Many problems occur when customers suggest *changes to a product*. Make sure they know as soon as possible the cost implications of making these changes. Give them a real figure – don't estimate for the sake of speed, but ask the relevant technician. Sometimes apparently easy changes can be expensive.

Clients sometimes suggest these changes because they are really needed, but not always. The suggestion can be more of an enquiry. I have seen huge ill feeling caused by semi-serious enquiries being taken seriously – the customer says in an idle moment 'Supposing the widgets were green …'; the supplier goes away and repaints them all, then sends in a bill; the customer refuses to pay …

Note that the customer is fully entitled to change their mind. They're paying. Don't resent these changes, as they are part of the process of making your offer exactly what they want. But always make sure the customer understands the cost implications of their suggestions.

If you do get stuck in one of these traps, negotiate your way out of it. Remember that in good negotiation, both sides win. Negotiators who flatten the opposition win – in the short term, but don't expect to do business with the losers again.

Other advisers

You will need other professional advice from time to time.

The basic principle in dealing with outside advisers is – don't let them charge too much. Consultants, lawyers, etc. seem to have outrageous cost structures, but this is not your problem. Talk to your mentor and to other entrepreneurs/cornerstones about who offers good and sensibly priced advice. Then go and negotiate with them.

It's also worth contacting your local Small Business Centre (located across Canada), who offer a range of free consultancy services. Some Centres are a lot better than others, but you can only really find out how good your local one is by trying it.

Premises

Getting proper office space is one of the biggest problems faced by seedling enterprises. But tough, it has to be done. Forget all the hype about electronic networks. Working from home is OK for a sole trader, but you are building a team, and there needs to be space that belongs to that team and has the unreserved 'feel' of business about it.

By far the best solution to the problem is to try and beg for some free office space. This may seem undignified, but there are plenty of organizations with spare space. Try and do some sort of deal with them. Your mentor may well know someone who can help. After all, all you need is a room and a couple of phone lines.

66 Getting proper office space is one of the biggest problems faced by seedling enterprises. 99

Do not worry about the look of the place. When you achieve world domination, then flash offices may be appropriate, but until then, clients visiting your premises don't want to come away thinking they are funding a luxury lifestyle. They want to see commitment, energy and excitement, not fish tanks and cherry wood flooring and mahogany cabinets. (I actually worked with an entrepreneur who insisted on having a tank of piranhas in reception. And yes, he more than once 'entertained' clients by chucking a goldfish into the tank ...)

In fact, wherever possible, you should visit the client, not have them visit you. This is not because you've something to hide, but because you can learn a great deal about a client from their premises. Is the office buzzing? If so, they will have plenty of needs; it's up to you to find them. Are the techies really that bright? Watch them at work.

So, as long as there are not too many cockroaches on your potential premises, go for it ...

Of course, after a while the free dungeon just becomes too small. But by that time, your business will be ceasing to be a seedling anyway. Once you make the transition from seedling to sapling, then you should get some new offices. Proper ones that you rent.

I talk more about the delightful process of renting large offices in the next chapter.

Furniture

Your free dungeon probably won't come with furniture. Check your personal inventory for desks, cabinets, and furniture. Make some calls, find out the cheapest supplier of second-hand stuff, then hire a van. Make a day of it. There is a certain romance to having a ghetto-like office. It makes celebrating success all the more fun.

Beware of any leases that contain furniture. This is always a hidden way of selling you the stuff at a vastly inflated price. Rent empty premises and fill them yourself.

Getting the phone sorted will be a lot less fun than the furniture. It's a prerequisite of taking free space that there is a working phone line, but the moment you start needing more or better lines, prepare for a war of attrition along the lines of the Siege of Stalingrad. All the phone companies seem as bad as each other on this. You just have to keep badgering them. Remind yourself that you aren't asking the phone companies a favour: you're a customer.

The intrapreneur

The intrapreneur, the entrepreneur who does it from inside the big company, has many advantages over the entrepreneur going it alone. Premises? The company will provide them. Finance? The company should set aside a budget for you. Distribution and manufacturing facilities should be available.

But though sections of it might be a little easier, your route to success is essentially the same as the entrepreneur's.

"The intrapreneur's route to success is essentially the same as the entrepreneur's."

You must find a mentor high in the company – right at the top, if possible. (A corporate mentor is often referred to as your 'sponsor', but their role is the same.) They will be essential to your project getting off the ground, and will continue to champion it when other people in the business start snickering at it – which, believe me, they will, either because it's not working, in which case they'll consider that resources are being wasted, or because it is working, and they are jealous.

You must also build a team: four cornerstones, individuals within the company with those core skills but who really believe in, and will bat for, your product. If you can't find all the cornerstones internally, think about finding them outside. They must be highly incentivized – one disadvantage you have over the solo entrepreneur is that you do not have 80 per cent of a business to offer to four talented, loyal team-mates. The main incentives you have to offer are a more fun, less corporate working environment and that old corporate goody of 'status within the company'. 'There goes Smith. He was one of the team behind the magic widget ...'

Just as the entrepreneur and their cornerstones have to, you must set about refining your product, getting a White Paper out once you make your first sale, only drawing up a Real Business Plan when you have some real business to plan.

Conclusion

Remember that evening chewing the fat with friends in the pub? So much has happened since then ...

You found a mentor. You got the four cornerstones in place (though Gemma in finance has only just joined full-time). You have trusted, carefully chosen professional advisers, who are offering a special deal because they hope you will stick with them as you grow. You've organized funding – you have accessed key people who have an interest in your business, a belief that it will succeed and even customers that are willing to pay in advance. You drew up a White Paper on the strength of that deal which enabled you to make three more sales. Recently you drew up a Real Business Plan, which features a growth scenario that feels both positive and realistic ...

Congratulations!

Now you must understand that your business is about to change its nature. You are about to take employees on – the beginnings of your dream team. You will delegate real responsibility to them: it isn't just five of you plus the receptionist and the gofer, it's about to become a much bigger enterprise. No longer a seedling, but a sapling.

The adventure continues.

The

sapling

enterprise

SLEEMAN

NOTORIOUSLY GOOD

SINCE 1834

SLEEMAN.CA

The next phase of your business' life covers the period when it grows from a 5-person business to one with around 20 people on board.

Why 20? I have no idea, but I found it another magic number, like 5. A number of companies surveyed by the authors (informally over a beer or coffee) agree that the whole nature of the company changed after they grew beyond 20.

Note that the key dividing line between the phases is the number of people in the company, not turnover, profitability or any fancy business ratio – another indicator of that profound truth that business is fundamentally about people.

In market terms, the fully grown sapling enterprise is a 'boutique'. It serves a niche market; its customers come by personal recommendation (and of course come *back*, again and again). Its style is personal, friendly, deeply committed: everyone in the business shares the vision, and is prepared to put in the hours and effort to realize it.

This kind of business can run successfully for years – though a word of warning: I have seen several 'boutiques' become too inward-looking and suddenly find themselves outflanked by new, hungrier opposition or stranded as the market moves on without them.

"The key dividing line between the phases is the number of people in the company, not turnover, profitability or any fancy business ratio.**"**

Below is a typical sapling organization chart.

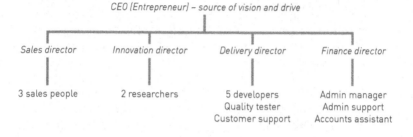

CEO (Entrepreneur) – *source of vision and drive*

Sales director	Innovation director	Delivery director	Finance director
3 sales people	2 researchers	5 developers Quality tester Customer support	Admin manager Admin support Accounts assistant

Naturally, you don't have to follow this pattern slavishly, but it's a useful guide to what the company could well look like once it reaches full sapling size. Note that this growth happens very fast once it begins. The butterfly analogy, with its implications of sudden quantum change, is actually better here: one day you were 5 plus assistants; 6 months later there are 20 in the team. Then you let it plateau out.

The sapling's growth period is a special time. The effort put into both people and culture lay the foundations for the future of the company; no matter how large it becomes. When the founders lose sight of their people OR get distracted by growth and/or bureaucracy, the company is certain to follow. Now is the time to develop activities that celebrate, recognize and embellish the people that give the company life. It may sound giddish (not sure that it is a word – but it feels right) but you are approaching a point where it can stop being fun. Make sure you take plenty of team photographs at different stages. A number of firms take pictures of every person as they join, and had them pinned up in a 'rogues gallery' in the office, along with a brief description of what they did, and an employee number. The latter related to when the individual joined, and became very important when the company got big. The good ones work very hard to integrate all people (new and old) from all departments at all times.

Whatever the precise shape of your organization chart, one thing is guaranteed. It will be hierarchical. You and your fellow founders aren't just running *and being* the business any longer, you're in charge of people. You're having to hire staff, to pay them salaries and bonuses, to lead them and motivate them.

You have become managers.

'Help! I wanted to get away from all this boss/underling stuff. All I wanted was to be with a great bunch of pals who believed in this wonderful idea ...'

Tough. There's no way a company can stay at five people; it either has to grow or (in the unfortunate and unusual case of a business that makes a few sales but never 'takes off') wither away. Later on, you may have a choice to stay a 'boutique' or to go for 'the big one', but there's no 'grow/no grow' choice at five people. It's grow or die.

So you're managers. Congratulations.

I may have forgotten to mention that people are the most challenging element in running a business. Each is different and must be treated different as one-size management practices does not fit all. They will dazzle you or they will disappoint you but often it is you that determines which occurs. Many people are put off 'management' by images of the old-style 'bastard boss'. But bosses like that have no place in the sapling organization – or any organization, in my view: if you've got a problem about your loveless upbringing or the size of your penis, go and see a therapist. Other people are put off management by shyness or lack of self-belief. To be honest, they're unlikely to be entrepreneurs or cornerstones, but if you do feel a little diffident about managing others – read on.

66 Grasp the challenge of management with both hands and really make it a creative expression of who you are and what you believe. **99**

The truth is that the basic management skills can be learnt. If I had to sum them up in two words, I'd say 'Take responsibility', and if I were given a sentence, I'd say: 'Have a clear, well-thought-out formal review process and care about the people below you'.

Enough to be getting on with for the moment? Grasp the challenge of management with both hands and really make it a creative expression of who you are and what you believe. That way you'll succeed, and enjoy it.

Culture and people

As I keep saying, business is ultimately about people. So the most important thing about running a sapling enterprise is getting the *culture* and the *individuals* right.

The culture of the sapling enterprise is tribal. Think chiefs and warriors (modern chiefs and warriors can be female as easily as male). Think close personal relationships. Everyone in the sapling company knows everyone else well. They all get on.

Impossible? No. It is an often said but seldom practiced expression that the key advantages of most successful firms are its people. This appears in oodles of mission statements only to be left as words on the wall.

Building a tribe of 20 people who are both excellent at their work and who get on socially is not easy. It might seem appallingly daunting. But it can be done. Believe in your ability to do it.

At The Instruction Set we would all go down to the pub most Friday nights. It was great fun, and I miss it a lot now. Sometimes, the session was totally unstructured (with the only rule that the managers buy the first round, and continue to be generous thereafter). Other times we had awards. These awards were, of course, very informal, though behind the informality a lot of thought had gone into who got the awards and why.

There were three basic awards. 'Mini Oscars' went to people who had done particularly special things that month – won a big contract, solved some particularly nagging technical problem, had been particularly praised by a client (or whatever). There was a 'Pranny of the Month' award for some mild balls-up like locking yourself out of your car or spilling coffee all over a report. Finally, 'Unsung Hero' usually went to someone quite junior who'd done something special.

These may sound a bit juvenile, but, believe me, they worked. The rather serious accounts assistant glowed with pride on being nominated 'Pranny of the Month': suddenly they had the right not to be so earnest, so quietly, dully perfect. The systems administrator – one of those jobs where you only get noticed when things go wrong – really did appreciate their 'Unsung Hero' award.

In other companies, I've been involved in team-building 'away-days', getting stuck on mountains or building rafts which, of course, collapse halfway over whatever sludge-bottomed piece of water you are supposed to be crossing. The secret of getting the most out of these is to mix teams – in other words have techies and sales people teamed together rather than in water-tight 'tech v. sales' competition. Also, show the team you care about these sessions by having them in company time, not at weekends.

A team-building exercise I found particularly useful was role-swapping. Get the techies to meet clients. Send the sales staff on a technical course. Efficiency experts might throw up their clipboards in horror at this, but the more everyone in the sapling business understands and appreciates what everyone else does, the better that business will run.

“The more everyone in the sapling businss understands and appreciates what everyone else does, the better that business will run.”

These formal exercises are useful – though, to be honest, I think the social events, no matter how casual, were more effective and enjoyable. And you only get a hangover next day, not hypothermia or cholera.

Incidentally, these social settings are a very good place to spot potential dissent. However good your hiring/culture management, dissenting cliques will spring up occasionally. These need to be nipped in the bud – not by firing dissenters but by talking to the individuals involved and getting to the bottom of what their problem is. Are there three people sitting in one corner, backs turned towards the rest of the team? It sounds obvious, but I've seen it.

Also, it's a sad truth that people do reveal different sides of themselves when they've had a few drinks. This can be used cynically, but shouldn't be. If someone expresses dissent over their fifth pint, don't take them to task for it next Monday. Talk about it; get the problem sorted.

Office romances may become more apparent in social settings too. Office romances spring up a lot in sapling enterprises. It's a sign that the culture is working: people are really getting close. In an ideal world, they wouldn't get *that* close, but these things happen. Go ahead and celebrate them – with the obvious proviso that the participants' work mustn't suffer.

I'm talking about romances between equals, of course. Unmarried equals, preferably. I know of companies where senior people have abused their position to pursue subordinates, and it is very damaging to 'tribe' morale. If you really do decide that the accounts assistant is the love of your life, then they will have to leave the firm. If you just fancy a casual fling with them, go and take a cold shower and act more maturely. (This may seem harsh, but it's called self-discipline. Note that it also protects you from the 'VP vampire' phenomenon, where a junior seduces a senior, acts so unreasonably that the senior is forced to end the entanglement, then hits them with a huge lawsuit.)

The truth is that office romance is out for the founding team. You can't pursue juniors, and romances with other cornerstones create terrible imbalances of power in the boardroom.

Recruitment

Recruitment is probably the single most important issue for the sapling company. Recommendations from employees remain one of the most effective and oft applied method of bringing people into an organization. When someone recommends a friend they put their reputation on the line. Welcome recommendations by getting everyone in the organization involved in it. Incentivize the bringing in of good people. 'I've got this friend who'd be just perfect for that job. I know they're not happy where they are at the moment ...' Brilliant!

A good culture really helps here. If your staff think that working for you is the best game in town, they will be eager to get people they like on board.

Think teenage kids and gangs and you won't be far wrong.

As the entrepreneur or a cornerstone, you are still in overall charge of the hiring process, however. You can't rely on new team members bringing in mates; you should always be looking for solutions to staffing problems yourself.

"Get everyone in the organization involved in recruitment."

Smart entrepreneurs understand the value of networking and use contacts unashamedly. Personal recommendations; people you've seen do a good job; friends. Our meritocratic business ethos frowns on this approach: images of old school ties and strange masonic handshakes come to mind. But for the sapling enterprise, trust and enthusiasm are key qualities, and it is simple common sense to look for these where you would look in ordinary life – among people you meet and like.

The only caveat is to watch out for cronyism by the entrepreneur. As you know, entrepreneurs are single-minded (to put it tactfully) and may try and surround themselves with sycophants or groupees – the type you see hanging round pop stars telling them they're cool every 10 minutes. I refer to these type of people as 'bobbing heads', you know those funny little spring mounted heads that are stuck on car dashboards. All they do is nod yes to every statement and idea presented by the entrepreneur. The best way to avoid this is to make each director responsible for hiring within their department. Giving everyone in the team a veto (see below) is another valuable and effective safeguard.

The alternative to hiring via contact is hiring by interview. Frankly, it is much more difficult to successfully hire through interview. Most young businesses simply do NOT have the knowledge or the resources to interview effectively. I would argue in favour of professional support. Perhaps one of your advisory board members (to be discussed later) has expertise in this area and can provide some guidance. In fact, the unseasoned entrepreneur and team might also be exposing themselves to potential liability if the interview is not managed professionally. A great deal should be invested in the hiring process to ensure you get the best person and avoid potential booby traps. Straight, open, fair – and highly problematic until you're a much bigger company with a proper HR department and proper HR procedures. The interview process may be open and fair, but not all applicants are. Having interviewed many individuals I continue to marvel at how good some are at presenting themselves in a very positive way only to discover that answering interview questions represents their only positive attribute. There are many ways to shift the advantage in your favour. Testing, situational questions (describe), cases and references all level the playing field somewhat. In the preliminary stages, make sure that you bring a number of people into the process. The potential peers and the manager are a minimum of who should be involved. Note however that peers should never approach an interview cold and unprepared. Another trick that has worked very well is to have the receptionist (if your firm has one) provide input after meeting and greeting the individual. While the person might be very cordial and professional to those doing the assessing – they may be quite the opposite to someone they believe is not a factor. I've seen candidate perform Jeckyll and Hyde like transformation between the way they behave when entering the business compared to that demonstrated during the interview.

Trust your judgement. And that of your colleagues.

When you do decide to hire somebody, introduce them to the rest of the team. Not just to the entrepreneur and the other cornerstones, but to everyone in the business. And if *anyone* expresses misgivings – don't hire the person. I consider the first day of employment the most important for the new employee. It is a make or break moment that either reinforces the decision they made to join the company or leaves them wondering whether they made a sound choice. I scoff at firms that don't invest heavily in this experience. Effective orientation is the gateway to a great work experience and a motivated employee. Of one thing it allows the employee to resolve all of the unknowns and let's them get to the task at hand – their job.

It sounds like a session from Bible School but treat others as you would like to be treated. If your idea of a good first day of employment is to be shown a desk and offered good luck... well, you shouldn't be a manager.

The new arrival should be on a six-month trial period. You should diarize some time three months into that period to talk with your fellow cornerstones about this person. Are they fitting in? Are they delivering what they said they would? The former is the biggest problem. 'Brilliant but disruptive' people cause more trouble than they're worth. Look out for signs of a poor temperamental fit:

- rude to junior staff
- poor timekeeping
- obsession with status
- long personal calls or lots of time on the Internet on irrelevant sites.

After three months, if they are not integrating then it's time for them to go.

But pick people well, get everyone to vet them, motivate them once they arrive – and you won't have to dismiss people. They won't leave, either, unless a major change of personal circumstances forces them to. To me, a hire-and-fire culture is the opposite of good business practice.

Dismissal

If you *do* have to dismiss somebody, it is infinitely better that they leave on good terms rather than bad. Most sapling enterprises operate in quite small business areas, and you don't want enemies out there gunning for you. Also, 'friendly dismissal' is in keeping with the tribal atmosphere of trust.

How can this be achieved? By making the dismissal process open and unambiguously fair.

There are two main reasons for dismissal; one is simple failure to do the job properly, the other misconduct. In both cases, there are correct procedures to follow. A paper trial must be maintained to ensure you are protected.

When someone has to go because of *poor performance*, then there should be a clearly understood pathway, which forms part of the appraisal process. A section on appraisal follows this one.

For *misconduct*, staff should get a verbal warning, then a written warning, before being dismissed. Some people say this is too soft, and cite silly examples of giving people verbal warnings for coming into work one morning and smashing the computers (or the computer operators) up with an axe. These counter-examples are not realistic: stick to this procedure.

The most difficult dismissal is of someone who has the ability and has been trying their best, but has been underperforming due to circumstances beyond their control. Examples: a partner or child has a life-threatening illness; the individual is hit by illness or depression. The first thing to do is to try and get help for them. If this doesn't work, there may have to be a parting of the ways, at least temporarily. A good manager will have procedures in place to help the employee through their challenges even if the person is being dismissed. I recall an employer who aided an addict by getting counseling and supporting as much as possible even though the person had been terminated. In addition to the humane way to treat people, it shows the compassion of the entrepreneur without accepting any inappropriate behavior.

It is best to have two meetings with the person being dismissed. The first is relatively brief. Explain that they have not achieved what was hoped, run through the formal aspects (warnings, missed targets); ask them if they really feel at home in their work. They may well be very honest about this, as they are secretly feeling guilty for letting the rest of the tribe down (though for some people, problems are always somebody else's fault). Then break the bad news. Offer a good severance package. Avoid personal criticism in all cases.

Some 'dismissees' threaten to get lawyers in. Fine. If you have followed my advice, you have stuck to both law and agreed company procedure, and thus have nothing to fear. Usually these threatened lawyers disappear once the departing individual gets a cost estimate from them.

There should be a second meeting, the exit interview, a while later. The person leaves, takes a break, comes to terms with what has happened, then comes back to tie up any loose ends. Agree to differ on any contentious points. Finalize severance agreements. Make the parting amicable.

Some enlightened companies actually try to find jobs for ex-employees: Accenture does this, with the result that it has friends in high places all over the business world. An obvious statement but worth noting is this extension of support should only be done when dismissing is not related to purposeful misconduct.

Appraisal

I've mentioned appraisal above, but want to look at it in greater depth, as it lies at the heart of good management. It should happen every six months: you sit down with each team-member and look at what they have done in that six months, at what they can learn from it, at what you expect from them in the next six months. At the same time, it's a good opportunity to get some feedback about how *you* are perceived, and to talk to the individual about the company in general – where it's going and how you see their role in that development.

If someone fails to meet the goals set six months ago, the best question to ask is what you can do to help them get it right next time. 'What do you need to do the job better?' is an infinitely better question than 'Why?', which just puts people on the defensive. Usually they will tell you what they need. Go with this, using your intelligence and intuition. For example, a salesperson says they've got a horrible client list. Is this an excuse or a real reason? If the latter, find some better ones for them.

"Appraisal lies at the heart of good management."

If their answer feels like an excuse, probe deeper. Sales staff often complain about props like the brochure, but this is rarely the actual problem: selling is about preparation, confidence and rapport, not brochures. Go with them on a visit; try to spot what they are doing wrong. It will often be something very obvious. If so, stay cool, point out the error and let them learn from the experience.

The same is true of technical staff. Get the relevant cornerstone to spend some time working alongside them, to see what they're doing wrong, and then help them sort it out.

Failure to meet a realistic target can be a sign of a weakness that can easily be remedied. If you don't set targets it's amazing how much you can miss. All of this is captured in the employee's file and reviewed semi-annually. The better the notes the easier the role of the manager and the less–likely to make critical mistakes.

Finally, remember that if there's an individual that you (and the rest of the team) really like, and who really likes the company, but who is underperforming, then consider if they might be of use elsewhere in the company. You are well shot of mediocrity and lack of interest, but passion that hasn't quite found its best medium of expression is like unrefined gold. Work on it.

The most important point in all of this is that a manager should be allowed to manage. This means giving the manager the resources (primarily time and training) to invest in their people. By overloading with report writing and other non-managerial duties they are neglecting their most important role and that is to enable the best performance and contribution from staff and subordinates. I would argue that the manager, in a proper context is really subordinate to the staff. In their capacity they should be working to ensure the team are provided the resources, clarity and the necessary feedback.

Leadership

I said earlier that you have now become managers, but what you have become is a *leader*.

Does that sound better?

Some of you will thrill at this thought. Others may shiver, as thoughts of Chairman Mao or Orwell's 'Big Brother' come into their heads. Forget these negative images. The truth is that leadership is a wonderful soul-expanding experience – if done in the right spirit, which is positive, adventurous and humane. People will love you for providing really good leadership.

"Leadership is a wonderful soul-expanding experience – if done in the right spirit, which is positive, adventurous and humane."

As a leader, your two main jobs are *strategic* and *motivational*. You have to work out where the business is going and decide on the best way of getting there, then get everybody else heading in that direction, too. In the sapling enterprise, strategy is the lesser of these two challenges: I talk a little about it later, but first, and most important, is ...

Motivation

What does actually motivate people? That's a classic 'How long is a piece of string?' question, as there are so many different sorts of people in the world. But we are only looking at the kind of people whom you need, and who will flourish, in the sapling enterprise. Your 'dream team'. I have a great deal of experience with such people, and know what they want.

Hint, it's not money. Not most of all, anyway. In descending order it is as follows.

Respect

Self and peer respect. They like the people they work with. They respect their colleagues and are respected by them. Outside working hours, they tell their friends they are working for your company, and expect those friends to be pleased for them, impressed and even envious.

Making a difference

Many employees of sapling enterprises come from big organizations, where they have felt swamped and irrelevant. They want to be involved in the making of decisions, and they want to know that their decisions and actions have a real effect. This is a gentler but still powerful version of the entrepreneur's passion for changing the world.

Challenge

Sapling employees are there for a challenge – to stretch themselves, to learn and grow. There is plenty of opportunity for this in saplings: there are always more things to do than people to do them. So if anyone has the balls to say 'Let me try', unless it's outrageously inappropriate, let them.

Advancement

If you're really into scaling ladders, you will probably go and join a big corporation, and scheme your way to an office with two telephones and a carpet one millimetre thicker than the person next door's. Life in a sapling enterprise is more about the challenge of the job than getting 'vice-president' on your business card. But there will be opportunities for advancement if the sapling grows into a mighty oak, and some people join sapling organizations with this clearly in mind.

Money

Of course it does matter, so pay people as well as you can afford. Give bonuses, too, but *not* individual ones – whatever any books on management, experts you meet in pubs (etc.) tell you. It simply isn't true that you can pay people wildly different amounts of money and they won't find out. They will, and the discovery of huge differentials will breed arrogance, demotivation, distrust ...

Individual bonuses go right against the tribal, team environment that drives sapling enterprises. You are all in this together, remember? Team bonuses are, of course, good things; given to everyone, based on the performance of the tribe as a whole.

"Everyone's salary and bonuses should be public knowledge."

I believe that everyone's salary and bonuses should be public knowledge. The sort of people you want to employ in sapling organizations aren't irrationally envious. They're quite happy for someone in the organization to be earning $300,000 per annum, provided they think that person is adding an appropriate amount of value to the team effort. Post salaries on the company intranet – why not? If anyone comes and asks why they are 'underpaid', explain why, and what they have to do to get paid better. And if your $300,000 person is clearly useless – I've worked with people getting twice this amount, who seemed to bring nothing to the party at all – then the more embarrassed and humiliated they feel at this, the better.

Such a policy encourages openness. It discourages overgenerous 'golden hellos' to people (often pals of the entrepreneur).

Stock options are another bone of contention. They're a great idea – in theory, but the idea was so abused back in the dotcom bubble that I now put them in my personal Room 101, along with arrogant MBAs, greedy VCs (etc.). In my view, stock options in sapling companies should be regarded as worthless. If you are seeking a job in such a company and they offer you a tiny salary but plenty of options, ignore the options and ask yourself if you are prepared to work for these people for the salary they are offering. Your answer may be 'yes', because they are great people with a great product, which is fine. If the answer is 'no', walk away.

Sapling stock options are usually illusions. As the company gets bigger and bigger, your stake does not grow, but shrinks because more and more options get allocated. In some cases early-granted options mysteriously disappear altogether, via some arcane refinancing package. It becomes legally possible but, given legal costs, actually impossible, to get these options back.

Entrepreneurs can start treating options like royal patronage, handing them out to all and sundry. This dilutes existing stakes, and can end up in a position where the company effectively has to cheat people. I know of one entrepreneur who promised over 100 per cent of his business in stock options!

There is a proper use for stock options, and I talk about this in the next chapter.

To return to our hierarchy of motivations, the least important ones are as follows.

Security

This is rather despised by the young go-getters who join sapling enterprises, but note that older employees start worrying about it. Older people can be very valuable in sapling teams, so bear this change of priority in mind.

Work environment

Many businesses start in the basement, spare bedroom or garage (the garage is not as likely a place to start a business in

Canada). I believe this is the stuff of legend. Reminiscing back to the early days of five nights of Kraft Dinner and a surviving in a grungy basement set up is endearing. By the standard of some start-ups, this would have embarrassed Louis XIV with its luxury. You should now be moving to new premises (see page 91), but they still won't be those marble-halled corporate temples the entrepreneur dreams of.

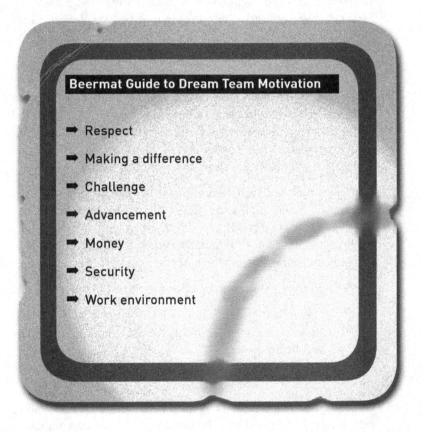

Beermat Guide to Dream Team Motivation

➡ Respect

➡ Making a difference

➡ Challenge

➡ Advancement

➡ Money

➡ Security

➡ Work environment

So that is the hierarchy of needs in the sapling enterprise. It's not that different from Maslow's classic hierarchy actually, with achievement and self-expression at the top and security and surroundings at the bottom.

There are natural parallels that can be drawn between the tribal sapling enterprise and some sports teams. The number of people involved is about the same as a sports team. The age profile of sapling employees is similar to that of most sports teams: young, energetic, 'up for it'. They are driven by a number of intrinsic factors. Sapling business really is a sports-team game, in a way that seedling isn't (too small), and the massive corporation, despite the endless corporate flannel about 'team-building', can never be.

"There really are only 20 of you, and it's you against the world. And it's bloody marvellous.**"**

There really are only 20 of you, and it's you against the world. And it's bloody marvellous, believe me!

The great sports leaders motivate their players in a number of ways ...

Understanding the individual

Sportsmen and women may seem super-competent, but they actually vary as much in temperament as employees. Some are plagued with lack of confidence: it's their undeservedly low self-image that keeps them practising and practising. Others have booming, overconfident egos: success comes to them because they know it will. Out on the field it may not be clear which person has which self-image. Give them the wrong kind of motivation, and it becomes apparent at once.

It is interesting to speculate how many people who appear to be underperformers are actually people whom nobody has taken the trouble to work out how to motivate. Of course, ideally we should all be self-motivators – if you are an entrepreneur, intrapreneur or cornerstone, you will be.

Not slagging off failure but learning from it

There's no point in getting at people for their failures. If somebody goofs, the need is for them, and the rest of the team, to learn from that mistake. Success should be dwelt on, failure shouldn't. It is important to point out that most successful entrepreneurial firms found success in their misfortunes and competitive advantage in their mistakes. The way to rise above mediocrity is often provided by mistake making and how they are addressed.

'Blame cultures' encourage people to put their own safety before the welfare of the group, to score cheap points off one another, and generally to avoid risk. Not what you want in an entrepreneurial business, or a sports team whose job it is to go out and win.

Note that our 'Pranny of the Month' ceremony in the pub was always carefully set up to be in a light, humorous spirit – a spirit of forgiveness and inclusion rather than of blame and exclusion.

Celebrating success

This gets drilled into sports teams, which is why you see macho footballers kissing and hugging each other after a goal. Your team achievements should be celebrated too, with days out, bottles of champagne at the office, meals, trips to concerts, movies. You are effectively writing the story of your company's success here, and the more clearly that story is embedded in everybody's minds via happy memories, the better.

Giving praise

Individual success should be celebrated, too – in public, which multiplies the motivational value of the praise many times. It's extraordinary how seldom people get praise from some bosses, even when the boss genuinely reckons that the work has been excellent. But there is no better way of motivating people (see 'Respect' above). Giving praise also sends out a general message: this is a place where excellence is encouraged and celebrated. I am not a fan of employee of the month awards. Employees who deserve recognition should not have to wait until the end of the month. The enlightened organization is quick to celebrate a great effort made by an employee. 'Employee of the moment' is never delayed but always enthusiastic. You can never have too many amazing moments or acts.

Being visible

This is hugely important. Leaders have to look positive. Good leaders never hide in the executive wing or create an environment where employees announce a 'boss sighting'. They should be engaging employees throughout the organization and reminding each of the company's mission and the important role the employee plays.

"As a leader you must give off positive vibes. All the time."

Visibility is also important in big companies: you won't be able to hide later on. John Chambers of Cisco Systems makes it a point to roam the company and give out treats. It is an old-fashioned but effective way of connecting with employees. Critics would complain about the choirboy approach to leadership or that he could better spend time. For John, it is one of a number of activities that have defined his role as CEO.

Staying positive

As a leader you must give off positive vibes. All the time. Whatever is happening in your personal life, or to the company for that matter. This does not mean 'tell lies about the state of the business', of course. It does mean stay positive and show it, all the time.

Generating enthusiasm

This is a job for the entrepreneur, and it really is a gift. You can't learn how to do this really effectively (though like all 'emotional intelligence' skills, you can improve those gifts that you have). Entrepreneurs do it naturally, their enthusiasm bubbling out all over the place and their commitment showing that they really mean it.

Leading from the front

Showing you mean it means leading from the front, it means being seen to be working as hard and as smart as your brightest employee. The old-style corporate manager who did a lot of 'work' on the golf course or over a long lunch may well still have a role in a big company – contacts are kept alive this way – but this is not a style that suits the sapling enterprise. The cornerstones remain the measurement of work ethic in the company. Leading by example is always important but never more so at this time. Employees that are new to the firm are heavily influenced by how the senior team behaves and works. My brother set the example by being the first in and last out of the office. His role has evolved since the Sappling days but he still wears his pride for the company on his sleeve and works hard at ensuring continued success.

Leadership on a Beermat

➡ Understand individual team members

➡ Celebrate success, learn from failure

➡ Give praise

➡ Be visible

➡ Stay positive, all the time

➡ Generate enthusiasm in others

➡ Lead from the front

➡ Set goals and monitor them

Setting goals

Leaders set goals. Goal setting is about having a vision of where an individual can get to, and about understanding the steps they have to take to get there. Well-set goals 'plot a path' to success via a series of challenging but achievable milestones. Sometime milestones are created from adversity. I recall hearing famed basketball player Michael Jordan address what drove success. "When I got cut from the varsity team as a sophomore in high school, I learned something. I knew I never wanted to feel that bad again. I never wanted to have that taste in my mouth, that hole in my stomach. So I set a goal of becoming a starter on the varsity." From: **I Can't Accept Not Trying: Michael Jordan on the Pursuit of Excellence.**

Strategic leadership

I said that leaders have two functions, strategic and motivational. In the sapling organization, the latter is more important than the former.

There is not too much complex strategic thinking to be done at this stage in the business' life. The aim, simply, is to grow. The means are:

- happy, motivated people
- carefully controlled costs
- delighted customers.

Not too much strategic wizardry there. At this stage you *shouldn't* be innovating that much: you have your core product, and though you will find yourself tailoring it to particular customers, you will not be altering it radically but always preparing to hear the 'growl' of the competition.

Business magazines are full of articles on creativity, the need for perpetual innovation and so on. But the sapling stage is an odd period when these actually don't matter that much. Your product must have been innovative to have got this far: right now creative thinking is about finding uses and markets for it.

The entrepreneur will still be thinking strategically, anyway. Entrepreneurs do. The cornerstones' job is to downplay this, and keep the enterprise focused on the job in hand. When you go for growth, and become a mighty oak, then strategy will come into its own.

Incidentally, I find it intriguing that strategy-speak often resorts to the imagery of war. There's a whole sub-genre of business books that wheel out classic military thinkers like Sun Zi (Sun Tzu in old-fashioned spelling) or Clausewitz and reinterpret what they teach for the business market. This may be relevant to great corporations, but I believe strongly that the sports field is an infinitely better metaphor and inspiration for the sapling business.

Sapling sales

I have talked about the aspirations that the seedling sales cornerstone should have: a portfolio of 10 to 15 customers, with 20 prospects in their sights. Of course, this is the ideal state of the sapling organization.

My model may appear too high-tech or service-orientated ('It's all right for people running Unix training courses, but we make widgets'), but I don't believe it is. Sapling manufacturers overwhelmingly sell to other businesses, either to other manufacturers or to some kind of channel to market such as the big retailers. If so, they are in exactly the same position as a high-tech company or service provider – you have big customers, and your job is to keep them convinced you meet their real needs better than anyone else.

For example, if you have a wonderful mineral spring in your back garden, you could bottle the water and sell it in the local market. If you want to build the business, however, this strategy won't work – you need an intermediary who will get the water to many more people. Who might this be? Retailers are the obvious ones, though they are pretty ruthless with small suppliers. Be more imaginative. Offices with thirsty workers? Caterers? You may need to think of clever ways of adding value to your product, providing the thirsty office with a dispenser which you undertake to fill regularly, or agreeing to provide the caterer with special bottles with 'Ethel and Fred, Silver Wedding' on. What all the above ideas have in common is that in each case your key sale will be to an individual in the relevant organization. Although you have a 'consumer' product, your key sales are business-to-business: the time for armies of reps, call centres, etc. is still a long way away (and may never be reached).

The only exception to this is a pure retail outlet, though even here a few large business contracts can make the difference between failure and success: a friend of Chris's who ran a bookshop made his money supplying local schools, not from walk-in customer. (Another key to success for the shop was the owner's ability to get it talked about by local opinion formers.)

In sapling selling nothing beats personal contact. Your sales cornerstone was selected because they are likeable, confident and a good listener. They should be using those traits now, to instigate, build and cement a continuing relationship with key customers. They should meet the client at least once a month and be in touch by e-mail once a week.

> **"Remember that in sapling selling nothing beats personal contact."**

These 'nudge' e-mails should be short and offer real value to the reader – information that may not change the world but that is relevant and interesting. 'Did you hear about XYZ's deal with BT?' 'Have you heard Jane Doe has left ABC?' If you can phrase it as a question, that increases involvement.

Telemarketing is also a useful tool at this point, maintaining your database of reserve potential clients (the 100 or so queuing up behind your 20 lead potential customers). 'Is Bill Smith still the purchasing director at ABC Grommets, and has his e-mail changed?' It's amazing how much information these calls can yield if the person at the other end of the line is chatty: if they're not, get the info and move on.

In dealing with new business, it is a good idea to get the entrepreneur involved early on, so they can work some of their charm and passion on the customer. Then get them out of the loop, or they'll start meddling. Towards the end of the negotiation, when things are getting to the 'nitty gritty' stage of bargaining over delivery times, payment schedules and so on, get the finance cornerstone to negotiate with the customer's purchasing director. At the end, the entrepreneur can reappear and thank the customer for their business.

Remember that in your Real Business Plan you had 10 customers in mind. When you actually have 10 customers (they may not be the originally planned 10), then you have leapt another hurdle. Well done!

Where should you look for quality leads? You can't beat promoting conferences and seminars. Such events are good general exposure for the company, and can be an excellent showcase for particular products. Make sure the events offer real benefits: get good external speakers and have really useful information on offer. That way people associate you with quality. You can also charge for the conferences and still get a decent turnout: 100 people is ideal, big enough to make the room look full, but small enough so that you can get your people to talk to each delegate. Half a day is long enough for most people's attention span. Offer a nice buffet lunch as a closer, and a free afternoon demonstration of your product at work. Anyone who stays behind for this is a serious potential customer. Offer them a free seminar on their site.

These targeted client seminars are the most effective account development tool I know – the equivalent to 100 sales visits in one day.

Telesales people are ideal for promoting these conferences. Use them. Of course, you should avoid telesales *direct to consumers*, which will make people hate you ('Hello, I'm Darren, and I know you're just about to sit down to a candlelit dinner with your partner but I wonder if you'd like to talk about double glazing for 10 minutes instead ...').

I love sapling enterprises, because I'm a salesman and because the fact is that *sales drive sapling enterprises*. Market instinct and technology drive the seedling; marketing and delivery drive the mighty oak; but the sapling grows by the oldest business art of all: good selling.

Problems and advisers

The seedling company needs a few good advisers, and the same is true of the sapling. In both stages, there is a premium on vision, passion and commitment. This is as it should be, but brings the potential downside of myopia. We all have a great capacity for seeing things as we want to – or as we expect to – which makes the objective eye of the trusted outside professional of enormous value.

However spot-on your vision and however masterly your execution, something will go wrong at some time. Probably several things will go wrong at several times, and every now and then several things will go wrong at once.

The first thing to do is 'ask the troops'. Get the opinions of the people at the coal-face: sales and technical. Together, have a careful think about what has gone wrong and why. Problems in sapling organizations nearly all come from quite simple sources. Here are some scenarios, and what to do if they arise.

- *You run out of cash.* Get selling, fast! I have more than once been told, 'If you don't sell something tomorrow, we're going broke.' It certainly concentrates the mind. However, it shouldn't really happen. The finance cornerstone should be watching cash flow like a hawk. They should have an imaginary timetable of 'how many weeks till the closing down party', and when that total gets low, everyone should be put on red alert. Sell more, spend less!
- *Costs out of control.* That's the other thing the finance cornerstone should be fixated with. Get pruning fast.
- *The bank withdraws the overdraft facility.* Talk. To your suppliers and customers, about temporarily adjusting payment terms.

To the bank, about the possibility of a loan to cover the new cash hole. To other banks, whose managers may have 'new account' targets to meet. To your team – ensure they understand the full gravity of the situation. To your mentor. To your life partner – they must understand this is a highly stressful time for you. Also, sell assets. If you employ people, some may have to go. Stay strong.

- *Too many products.* This can happen if you over-customize, making sales unprofitable. Yes, very early on you should customize in order to find out what different types of customer want. Once you have established a typology of customers and created a range of products to suit them, stick to this range. The sales cornerstone may not like this.

- *Downturn in market.* A popular excuse for failure, but a bad one. Great companies survive the inevitable ups and downs of markets, and you are building a great company. The obvious answer to this problem is to 'work harder and smarter'. But also consider that market downturns can be opportunities. Are some of your less fit competitors going to vanish? Supplies – and more important, quality people – will be cheaper.

- *Rival produces a better product.* Make an even better one! You have some leeway: your customers won't change at once. They like you; what they want to hear from you is, 'Yes, that is a great new product. But we're going to beat it – just watch.' It's also true that amazing new products can develop glitches: don't panic, just put your innovation team on overdrive.

- *Rival produces an 'order of magnitude' better product.* (For example, what happened to Hoover when Dyson's cleaner came out.) This is a really tough one. Be very nice to your customers, to buy time. Get innovating fast. Look for 'cracks' in the super new product: few innovations are so perfect that there isn't some loss in changing from the old one to the new. If you find such a loss, play on your remaining advantage. Don't indulge in 'dirty tricks', both because you should have better ethics than that and because when the truth comes out, people will despise you for it. Ideally, of course, you'd have your finger on the pulse of the industry so you can see these innovations coming.

- *A rival tries to buy market share.* Talk to your customers. Try to find out if your rival has a real cost advantage (if they have, then try to match it) or if the price-cutting is pure aggression. In most markets, buying share is a short-term strategy that often rebounds on the price-cutter. Customers know perfectly well what the outcome will be – a near-monopolist who will suddenly turn round and ramp prices back up – and are distrustful of this kind of ploy. But they need reassurance from you. Their FD has been muttering about costs ... They will probably buy a few rival widgets and try them out. Your product should be better, so should see off the opposition. Of course, if you have a product that's worse and more expensive, you shouldn't be in the market anyway!

- *A key person in your business wants out.* Let them go; talk to your mentor about finding a quality replacement. This is more commonly a problem in mighty oak companies, and I talk more about this issue in the next chapter.

- *Irregular flow of orders.* A problem often faced by small businesses – a big order comes in; all hands to the pump; maybe you take on extra hands; the order is delivered ... then it all goes quiet. This is the 'feast or famine' phenomenon. It is essentially a sales management problem: the sales cornerstone should have a systematic pipeline of sales, and be moving potential customers up that pipeline all the time.

- *'Overtrading' – orders flow in, but cause delivery and cash-flow problems.* As a sales person, it breaks my heart to hear about this. If the marketplace is biting your arm off for your product, this is a *huge* win. So many great-sounding products don't sell: an unexpected level of real customer demand has to be good news. But it clearly does create difficulties elsewhere in the organization. I'm afraid this means late nights at the office for the delivery and finance cornerstones, and the entrepreneur, too. Get networking; get thinking fast on who you could team up with to get the delivery issues sorted. When you get a new and workable delivery plan in place, your bank – with whom you have a good relationship, remember, because your finance cornerstone keeps them up to date with your financial state – should be prepared to lend to you on the basis of a bulging order book and that plan. Incidentally, it's worth examining your internal communication if the 'overtrading' problem does arise. Didn't the sales cornerstone have clear targets, agreed by the board and in line with the business' plans? The moment sales began to exceed targets, why were the rest of the team not informed? Yes, orders can suddenly flood in, for example after an unexpected piece of publicity, but a much more common scenario is that the problem is allowed to build gradually because people have stopped talking to one another.

- *A supplier suddenly lets you down.* Obviously, try to negotiate *some* kind of delivery from them. But assume the worst. Don't waste time being angry – although you've a right to be, you have more important things to do! Work with the sales and delivery cornerstones to schedule what you can still deliver and what orders you will have to delay. Talk to the latter group of customers at once, and explain what has happened. If your sales cornerstone has been doing their job properly, they will like you and be understanding – for a while. This gives you a window of opportunity to source new supplies. Get networking. Talk to all your contacts – including your customers – to find out as much information about alternatives as possible. Talk to your mentor and set them networking too. Of course, the best remedy for this is to have alternative suppliers on hand. Just as your sales cornerstone has a list of 'prospects', your delivery cornerstone should have a list of 'prospective suppliers'. If possible, you should be sourcing some stuff from them already.

In all emergencies, obey these golden rules.

- Don't panic ...
- ... but do prioritize.
- Get the team together and work on the problem together.
- Gather as much information as possible as quickly as possible.
- Network!
- Leave the emotions (anger, blame, guilt, etc.) for later.

- Once you have decided on the way out, act quickly and decisively.

And when facing any problem, remember that all ventures encounter unforeseen difficulties (someone once described them as 'elephant traps' – one moment you're walking happily along, the next you're at the bottom of a large hole). Successful businesses scramble out of the traps. They can even benefit from the experience: the team is stronger; useful lessons have been learnt about how to deal with certain problems (and, sometimes, about who your friends really are); an episode has become part of the company culture. 'Do you remember that time when …?'

Remember, if you are sitting at the bottom of an elephant trap, that businesses also encounter the opposite: lucky breaks. (Two great questions to ask successful entrepreneurs are 'What was your worst moment?' and 'What was your luckiest break?' You'll get some fascinating answers.) I used to enjoy playing Snakes and Ladders as a kid, and still think that's as good a simulation of business life as those complex games beloved of management trainers.

"Remember that all ventures encounter unforeseen difficulties – 'elephant traps."

If you have been through all the possible obvious solutions, talking them over with the team, your mentor, your non-execs and anyone else whom you respect and who is prepared to give you free advice, and you're still baffled, maybe it is time to call in outsiders. As at the seedling stage, don't let them overcharge. I've been appalled by some of the work I've seen from big-name consultants, not because it was bad, but because of the price tag attached.

I also hate consultancy work, with any price ticket, that's in fluent management-ese. The philosopher Wittgenstein said 'Everything that can be said can be said clearly', and that should be the motto of all business communication.

Finance

Just as at the seedling stage, avoid external finance if you can. The best way to finance a sapling business is through cash flow.

- Keep the orders flowing.
- Keep the customers paying on time.
- Keep outgoings as low as possible.

A bank overdraft can cover working capital, and the purchase of income-yielding assets can be financed by loans timed to last the life of the asset, but otherwise avoid getting into bank debt. Your business is growing now, and should not be financed by ever-increasing debt secured against your personal property.

Keep watching expenditure. Growing companies may feel 'richer', but you still cannot afford to throw money around. The pantomime of govworks.com, a 'start-up' that burned its way through the best part of $42 million, should be a lesson to us all, with contractors and 'consultants' charging absurd fees and staff flying first class all over the world.

At the same time, of course, beware false economies. Outmoded technology, inefficient support staff, crummy business cards (or no business cards at all) ... There is always a fine line to be drawn. The best way to draw it is to make the people spending the money have to convince a sceptical financial cornerstone that the expenditure really is necessary. If they make a good enough case, a cheque is drawn. If they don't make out a good enough case, they get a reasonable explanation.

"However exciting your product, bright, motivated people will not come and work for you for peanuts."

One area where economies are almost always false is people. However exciting your product, bright, motivated people will not come and work for you for peanuts. Pay a little over the going rate, and monitor their progress carefully to make sure they are delivering value for money.

Continue to move heaven and earth to finance your business from cash flow.

PR/media

PR is a useful tool, but matters a lot more for some businesses than others. If you sell to the public, PR is very helpful. If you sell to business, your networking and word-of-mouth reputation are more important: highly credible companies need also be highly visible if they are going to leverage the company reputation.

So, first, make a decision – are we going to spend time on PR or not?

If you are, don't throw money at it. Beermat companies get free PR by providing well-chosen news media with real news (not 'look at me I'm wonderful' press releases). Establish contact with those freelance journalists whose names appear regularly in the relevant *specialist* or (if your market is local) *local* press. If you have a story, pitch it to these people, who, if they like it (i.e. if they agree that it is a real story, not just 'look at me'), will pitch it to the publication. By contrast, most press releases sent directly to publications go straight into the bin.

If you have a well-known customer who is happy with your work, see if their PR department will work with you on a case study. These are the stories that the publications really want – not dull product releases, but genuine customer stories of nasty problems neatly solved (by you, of course!).

The *mass* media are much more risky to deal with. They can enjoy building people up then knocking them down. You do not want to get involved in that process. People like Alec Baldwin seem to be able to emerge grinning out of it, but most people don't. Entrepreneurs like Michael Copeland, who was made a hero for Corel Draw then knocked down when he attempted to better Microsoft while making unsuccessful ventures in other developments. Research in Motion's Jim Basillee whose media image soared and plummeted with several failed attempts to acquire an NHL team while RIM's market and share price plummeted. Both would really have been better off if they'd never seen a reporter. As would Tiger Woods though as a sportsman, he had little choice in the matter. You do have that choice, and should exercise it in favour of caution and quietly getting on with your job.

Note that earlier I said that leaders should be 'visible'. I meant, of course, visible within the world of the organization and its customers, not to the sensation-seeking world out there.

Naturally, one person will disagree violently with the above: the entrepreneur. They can't wait to get into the press – specialist, national, whatever – telling the world about themselves and what they've achieved. Steer them towards the specialist and/or local press. This is less glamorous (so the entrepreneur may well get bored), more responsible and better targeted.

Law

Here again, there is no real difference between seedling and sapling. Don't take on specialist legal staff. Keep legal expenditure down by using boilerplate contracts. Above all, stay well away from the courts.

Now you have more contracts to watch, there is more opportunity for things to go wrong, so stay alert and keep talking to your customers.

Employment contracts will start to matter. The 'boilerplate' rule still applies: keep them simple. And remember that, while contracts are necessary, the most important part of an employment agreement is unwritten and 'psychological': you're recruiting members of a tribe, and legal niceties are largely irrelevant to this.

Premises

I said that one of the first things you do as a sapling company is move to your own premises. This is a special moment.

Finding the premises is rather less special.

For starters, it brings you into contact with commercial real-estate agents, another candidate for my Room 101. Arguably, they're the worst of the lot, as they tell lies. I know I'll get letters from the professional body whining, but I'm sorry, it's happened to me.

Commercial Real-Estate agents will also send you to ridiculously inappropriate properties, presumably to convince the property's owner that they are on the case. I'm sorry to be negative about a group of people who come in for a lot of stick, but they deserve it. If any commercial estate agents are reading this – clean up your act!

Please keep in mind that some commercial real-estate agents do represent the interests of the customer. I talked with several business owners who were very pleased with the level of service, the value of their insights and their knowledge of the market. The true professionals assist you in making better decisions and add to the excitement of the experience.

The entrepreneur also becomes totally infuriating while you are seeking premises. Premises are an expression of the business, and the business is an expression of their ego – so they immediately drop all the useful work they are doing in staff motivation and business development, and set off on a personal mission to find the perfect office. They abandon their desk; their mobile is permanently switched off; you're about to send out a search party, when they waltz into the office saying they've found exactly what the business needs. This will turn out to be horrifically expensive and, amazingly, five minutes walk away from their own home, though impossible to get to for everyone else.

There's only a little you can do to mitigate this. Chaining the entrepreneur to their desk might work, but they'll escape through the window when you let them go to the restroom. The only practical solution is to get someone whom the entrepreneur trusts to draw up a short-list of properties, then send the entrepreneur round these.

Note that the comments I made in the previous chapter about simple premises are still valid. The entrepreneur may want something grand, but your customers won't respect you for it. As my former lawyer suggested (at over $200 per hour), apply the KISS principle: Keep It Simple, Stupid.

When the entrepreneur has decided – and it really is best to let them decide – get your lawyers on to the lease. The cornerstones should visit, too, but nobody else, or you'll get endless arguments about commuting distances.

" The entrepreneur may want something grand, but your customers won't respect you for it. Stay simple. "

Someone will have the lovely job of ensuring the place fits Health and Safety regulations. These need to be taken seriously, as Health and Safety Inspectors can close you down if you are breaching these regulations.

You also need to consider security. Think like a burglar for a moment, and imagine how you might get in. Talk to the local police. You must have an effective and appropriate alarm system – though this will inevitably cause trouble at some time, going off at three o'clock one morning for no reason.

At the moment, the biggest security problem for small businesses is laptops. It's almost impossible to police a busy start-up enterprise, where people are always coming and going. However many badges your receptionist pins on incomers, someone will sneak in sometime. Make it a habit for all staff to lock their laptops to their workstation. It is an easy accessory to purchase and highly effective.

You can get laptop insurance, and this is worth shopping around for.

When laptops do disappear, the hardware is only part of the loss. You should guard against theft (and other computer-borne disasters) by backing all your machines up at least once a day. Get a good systems administrator to ensure this happens.

But don't lose sleep over security. Get the basics right, and get on with business.

When you finally move into your new home, make a party out of it. Have all the staff line up outside the entrance and have photos taken. Lay on some champagne and food inside – even bring music (don't leave this to the part-time janitor who says he's got an amazing sound system, and who turns out to like nothing but heavy metal). Celebrate!

This place, for all its drawbacks, is going to be very, very special.

Marketing

Strategic marketing involves looking at huge ranges of consumers and breaking them down into reasonably predictable groups that have similar purchase/consumption patterns. You started doing this when you asked 'Who will buy this?' the first night in the pub. The entrepreneur should still be thinking about it now, even though, if you have followed my advice, you should now be an expert on your key markets as you grow through the sapling stage. Strategic marketing is at the heart of business.

Less central is the stuff marketing communications companies try to sell you: brochures, newsletters and so on. I don't believe that saplings need these things, any more than they need expensive market data: you're not attacking a whole market yet.

Saplings need a crystal-clear vision of what they do and how that benefits customers, and likeable, efficient sales people who understand that vision and communicate it, person to person. And, OK, to back that up, they need certain 'market communication' basics – proper business cards, proper notepaper, a simple user-friendly website. Nothing more.

When the company grows beyond the sapling stage, when they have decided that they want to (and can) take a whole market by the scruff of the neck and conquer it, then more marketing paraphernalia will be required.

Which brings me nicely to...

The big decision – 'boutique or big one?'

As I've said, you can function as a sapling 'boutique' for a long time. Twenty people, really committed to the vision and its realization. Happy customers. A reputation for excellence ... It's a fantastic way to be in business.

As your reputation builds, nice things start happening, like:

- quality people start sending you their CVs
- bankers and VCs start contacting you, offering loans, money for equity stakes, etc.
- the press ring up for comment on developments in your area
- foreign buyers get in contact with you. This is equivalent to another hurdle crossed.

However, it is also a time to start asking yourself if you should consider further growth.

If your company grows further, its nature will change radically – whether you want it to or not. I guess it's to do with the psychology of how many people one can really know well and trust.

Beyond around 20 people, the organization of the business *has* to become more bureaucratic. The way you hire staff changes, and the way you motivate them changes. You may find yourself needing bigger premises: another culture change. The kinds of business done by the company seem to change as well. You need bigger income flows – and can get them. But in getting these, you are probably emerging out of your niche and flexing your muscles to take on all-comers. The big players start noticing you, and they don't usually hang out a sign with 'Welcome' on it. Once you have left your niche, it is almost impossible to scuttle back.

> **❝If you grow beyond the sapling stage, you must do so as the result of a positive decision.❞**

If you grow beyond the sapling stage, you must do so as the result of a *positive decision*. You must accept you are entering a new phase in the life of the business, and plan accordingly.

I have worked with start-ups that drifted beyond saplinghood into a kind of limbo, where they still wanted to operate – and feel – like a boutique, but just couldn't. Old hands started complaining, 'The company isn't like it used to be' and 'Nobody listens to me any longer'. Newcomers didn't know who everybody in the firm was ... These businesses didn't last long in this state: either they grasped the nettle and went for growth, with all its accompanying costs, or they fell apart.

Moving on can be a painful experience. Big companies are a lot less fun than small ones. There'll be more stress. And ironically, people feel a lot lonelier in them. I think our ancestors did live in little groups, and there is something about life in the small company that resonates with this evolutionary heritage. This vanishes once you go for growth.

Is there any alternative? Well, you can start turning down orders, and try to become a rather exclusive boutique. Or you can 'clone' – set up a model of yourself in another country. (This is not the same as growth: the end product is not a great, multinational 'oak' but a series of essentially independent saplings in different countries.) Cloning sounds an easy option but isn't: no two business cultures are the same, and a formula that works wonders in the UK may fail dismally in France or the USA. If you must clone, involve local people.

If you go for growth, you should end up with a substantial financial reward: you will work incredibly hard in an environment that is not really your natural one, but hopefully not for more than four or five years, at the end of which you will not need to work again. Or, more likely, you can go back to start-ups again, now safe financially.

It will be one hell of a challenge. Can you really turn it down?

The entrepreneur will have no doubt: they set out to change the world, and this is just another step on the road to achieving that goal. Oh, and they'll get the posh HQ and the media attention, too.

The cornerstones should be more thoughtful. There are five key criteria by which to judge their suitability to grow.

- *The market.* You must believe you have the ability to conquer a marketplace. By conquer, I don't mean monopolize, but become a market leader with a market share of about 30 per cent, or at least a fighting number two. Most mature markets have oddly similar structures. There's a leader, with that 30 per cent share (or thereabouts). There's a number two, with about 25 per cent, locked in battle with the leader (think Pepsi). Player number three specializes more, and has about 10 per cent. Other players occupy niches of various kinds. (There are exceptions, of course – natural monopolies – but not that many. Even Bill Gates is still battling with Linux.) The market you intend to conquer will probably end up in this standard shape – if it doesn't at the moment, this is probably because the market is immature. You must believe you have what it takes to end up in positions one, two or three as it matures.

"You must believe you have the ability to conquer a marketplace."

- *Sales.* You must have a regular flow of sales, from a wide range of customers. You leapt over another hurdle when you successfully delivered to your first 10 customers, but you are now casting the net even wider. Sometimes your customers actually ask you to grow. Sometimes they beg you to. If they really like the service they get from you, they will want more of it than a mere sapling can provide. In this case, you have very little choice, as if you don't offer them your product on the scale they have started to require, they will be forced to go elsewhere and find someone who provides something similar in the way they want it.

- *Organization.* You should have an efficient, established infrastructure with day-to-day tasks like payroll, delivery, security, etc. under control.

- *Finance.* You should have a healthy credit rating. How much can you borrow?

- *People.* This is probably the most important criterion of all. The 20 people that are your business must be crystal-clear about how they feel about making the change.

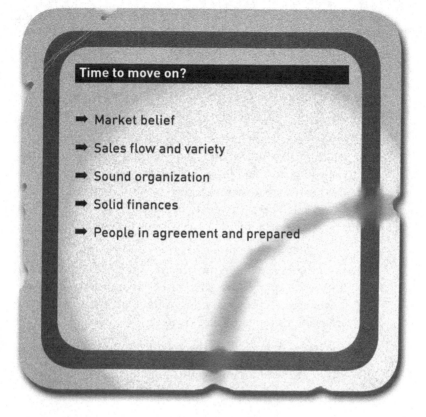

Time to move on?

➡ Market belief

➡ Sales flow and variety

➡ Sound organization

➡ Solid finances

➡ People in agreement and prepared

The best way to ensure a successful transition from sapling to growing oak is to confront the team with the decision a long time before it happens – when your staff level gets to 14 or 15. 'Some time in the future, we'll be faced with this choice. What do you think about it?' That way, when the crunch time comes, they'll be clear about which way they want to jump. And that's what you need: 20 clear decisions.

OK, if everyone apart from you says 'no', you've got a problem. If the five founders are divided, you've got a problem. But the most likely outcome is that most of the tribe will be up for it.

Those who aren't convinced are not to be banished, not to be airbrushed out like Trotsky from Soviet pictures. The growing company is developing a mythology, and anyone who was one of the original dream team has an inalienable and permanent place in that mythology. Give them jobs that feel as much like sapling jobs as possible: jobs without much line responsibility, jobs like selling into new, exotic markets or running the skunkworks.

Those who are up for the change must brace themselves for a change in work style. They are about to become managers in an organization that is colder, more bureaucratic.

When you decide to change, draw up a new business plan. This plan, which I call your Market Conquest Plan, looks like the fantasy business plans that blossomed in the dotcom era – only it's real. Real sales, real markets, real targets that you actually expect to meet. There are plenty of websites offering template business plans (including, of course, www.beermat.biz): now is the time to use them.

Drawing up a Market Conquest Plan is the ideal way to end your time as a sapling. You should feel in your bones that the plan is workable – you really do understand the market, you really do know your potential customers.

The tribe is about to move off the savannah into the first towns.

Life will never be the same again.

The

mighty

oak

In the first edition of this book, I argued that this new, third stage lasts up to any size to which the company grows. Once you get beyond 20, formal procedures have to be introduced. New people are employed who lack the spark and commitment of the dream team. The fun is over ... I still do believe that, as does almost everyone I meet who has built a company.

Maintaining the entrepreneurial spirit that brought the company to the Mighty Oak stage becomes a major challenge.

I would like to draw from the experience and wisdom of Peter Halsall. Peter is the current champion guiding Halsall and Associates, an innovative engineering firm. His father, Robert Halsall founded the practice in 1956 to provide clients with personalized engineering services. Since then, Halsall and Associates has grown to include more than 300 employees in six offices across Canada with a wide set of service offerings. The company's dedication to its employees has resulted in Halsall being recognized as one of the country's "Best Workplaces": year after year by the Great Places to Work® Institute of Canada.

"The book is about a company that wishes to retain the entrepreneurial spirit. That spirit has to be nurtured in the Mighty Oak stage. An entrepreneurial enterprise intends to generate new products or services to sell on a continuing basis, not just harvesting the idea or position that the company has established its current market presence with. A company designed to harvest an idea probably requires shifting to a significantly different paradigm than what the Entrepreneur went into business for. The question becomes how can you maintain the feeling of "the buzz, the spirit, the tribal adventure" when you are spending your time creating processes and managing people.

The entrepreneurial buzz in a mighty oak setting can come from the people side of the business, more than the idea generation. This requires changes both in people and in business focus. The entrepreneur and cornerstones in particular will have to want to change from working together developing an idea to developing a group who create an increasing range of ideas. The group development becomes the entrepreneurial idea. The members of the group are inspired by the entrepreneur and cornerstones in ways that meet their career expectations. The tactical process involves developing the range of skills needed to create balance as the idea(s) become reality. They find their needs being met by realizing the full value presented by that core idea and set of beliefs.

To manage a larger operation, the gang of 5 has to think about what personal changes they need to go through to achieve leverage, and accept the responsibility or move on (retire/sell/be responsible for less than the entire business).

To move into that Mighty Oak paradigm, the entrepreneur has to decide if they are motivated by the responsibility for getting lots of people to succeed, and be clear about how you aim to achieve it. There are usually significant changes required of the person. If the original mentor is more about the needs of the seedling or sapling stages, it is time to find one suited to the leadership associated with the mighty oak stage. If the motivation and skills line up, then size should not matter that much. Of course your model may not get you to a size that creates a problem.

The rule of 150 should probably govern the structure no matter what the total enterprise size. The units that people work in should probably not get larger than 150 to keep people most effective."

I don't want to terrify readers pondering the grow/stay small decision. If you go for growth, your business won't change into a faceless bureaucracy overnight. The changes are real, but subtler than that. If you are prepared for those changes, you can still make your 'young tree' business an enjoyable place to work.

Returning to Peter Halsall, "The company's sapling stage lasted for about 30 years delivering a boutique service. It grew to a maximum size of 90 people. It had the entrepreneur and 4 cornerstones in place. The cornerstone membership changed through the years, but the entrepreneur and 3 of the original cornerstones were still there in 1995. The company never had a mentor. To some degree once the company created a comfortable living, it was serving its purpose and the drive to innovate was limited to what was needed to stay current in the market. The cornerstones were all engineers, rather than specialists. Each took on a separate role – two of which were somewhat aligned with the Finance and Delivery tasks. Sales and innovation stayed with the entrepreneur. Growth until the 80's was achieved primarily by keeping up with a growing market for its service.

In the 80's, the entrepreneur realized that the market for dealing with existing buildings created an opportunity to grow the business. He hired an *intrepreneur* to lead this. This new business was developed in parallel with the existing business, but it started to fray the relationships between the entrepreneur and the original cornerstones who were less comfortable taking the business into new markets. The *intrepreneur* became a member on the cornerstone team, and developed a much younger Dream Team. Over time, the new business success created tension between the Entrepreneur and the original cornerstones. This tension became the basis for a transition in management from the original cornerstones to a new group, The Intrepreneur became President, and the cornerstone group changed with members from the younger dream team taking on key roles in the management structure. The original Entrepreneur became the mentor. This transition set the stage for going from Sapling to Mighty Oak.

A clear Mission and set of Core Values were agreed on to guide growth. There was a decision to focus on being "A company that we would be proud to have our children aspire to work at".

Since being Best of Market in our Services was inherent in the business from the beginning, it was a natural element of the Mission. We added a focus on creating Great Careers and Continuously Getting Better to the Mission. We also realized that to create great careers, we would have to provide a steady supply of new opportunities for people who wanted to increase in their responsibilities. This led to adding Sustainable Growth as the 4th element of the Mission.

An outside Board of Advisors provided reflection on the business that a mentor might have done. They advised that if we were to have such a focus on people, we needed to hire a professional human resources person to assume responsibility for this area. It took a few attempts before arriving at the right CFO and HR (we call it Career Development) director. We were clear about what we wanted in terms of understanding the mission and culture, but nailing that in an interview turned out to be tough. It was important not to settle for someone who was not going to support the growth.

The foundation for growth worked. The new managers were supported by the professional administrators. A list of opportunities for managing new business incubators was posted on the intranet for people to see what they could take on. It set the expectation that we wanted to support growth for current employees. It was not about hiring new people to start new parts of the business. But that happened. Once someone new became accepted as part of the "tribe", they were as eligible as anyone else for taking on new positions.

When it became evident that the last remaining member of the original Cornerstones was not as committed to the Best Careers and Sustainable Growth agenda, we moved a younger manager into his position. The significant growth that occurred in that part of the business created a whole new atmosphere, which the Cornerstone became a part of, but not responsible for." Peter Halsall

The number 150 may well be another milestone, though I think it is much less significant than 5 or 20. See Malcolm Gladwell's

The Tipping Point (Abacus, 2002) for a discussion of this number, which he reckons is the maximum size for a community of people who can have a 'real social relationship' with one another. (He cites many examples, and even an anthropologist who worked out a precise figure for this – 147.8!)

The period of growth from 20 to 150 people is one of balancing old and new. You are putting in systems, while trying to keep parts of the old culture – the memorable team building and fun activities, the effort to make recognition an event, even the occasional pub nights.

It is important to build effective processes and the firm may have to accept the inevitable intrusion of 'managed' bureaucracy, but at the same time finding ways to still have fun (though not nearly as much fun as when there was a small team of 15). It takes a concerted effort (but natural) in a unique type of culture to keep a spirit resembling 'fun' in the company. It requires a unique, almost quirky type of leader to promote happiness and fun in the workplace. I know of one small company who's boss did not permit laughter as he thought it inhibited productivity. Sufficed to say, the place stunk.

Westjet has developed a loyal following primarily by allowing its unique culture to flourish. This quirky corporate behavior promotes fun and personality (a far cry from the many airlines where you feel more like freight). It would appear hard to manage in a company as large as Westjet however they continue to maintain a loyal employee base, and build markets due to the continued presence of early and engrained principles.

Westjet, it would seem, continues to insist on a particular type of employee; someone with a sense of fun and an openness to change.

If you have enjoyed this book so far, you may not believe you are cut out for life in this new phase of the business' story. All those rules and conventions are what you joined a start-up to get away from!

Your belief about this may not be right. Some people make the change with ease. They are sharp enough to see the change coming, and they treat it as a whole new adventure. 'Right! Now I'm going to learn how to be a corporate manager!'

Others are wise enough to know they won't enjoy this, and retreat to the sidelines and hire specialist managers. If they do this, they must let these people manage, and not meddle – they must not commit the error of 'getting a dog and barking themselves'.

"The worst option is to ignore the change to oak, and pretend things are going to muddle along as before."

As with most changes, the worst option is to ignore the change to oak, and pretend things are going to muddle along as before, really. This is the Peter Pan syndrome, named after the little boy who never grew up. (He must have been a real pain to work with ...)

Whichever option they take, the oak stage will be a time of reflection for entrepreneur, cornerstones and dream team alike. Before, they all knew what they were in business for. They did it for the buzz, for the challenge, for the tribal adventure. But now things are changing ...

OK, they're going to make boat-loads of money, but that was never their number-one motive anyway. In the bigger, oak-organization, those tribal joys disappear, and money looms ever larger. Salaries are bigger, as are expense accounts, and for entrepreneur and cornerstones a giant cheque is appearing on the horizon if they decide to go down particular exit routes.

I talk more about exits later, but now an overview of oak life is needed. It will be briefer than my comments about seedling and sapling enterprises, because most management books are about oak organizations. They don't say *everything* about this phase, however ...

People, culture

One thing remains constant, at least – business is still essentially about people. But just as your dream team players were different from your four fellow founders, you will be recruiting different sorts of individuals into the growing oak. You will have a different, more distant relationship with them, too.

You are now taking on a fourth type of person (after entrepreneurs, cornerstones and dream-teamers): *employees*. Employees are usually specialists. They are unlikely to feel the same level of loyalty to the company; instead, they are selling you their skills at the market rate. So buy those skills, treat the vendors fairly and don't expect the kind of commitment you got from the dream team.

The employees' motivational hierarchy will appear different from the one I discussed in the last chapter. It probably isn't different in fact, but you only see a section of that hierarchy at work. They will meet their higher needs elsewhere or, if they do try to meet higher needs at work, it will be via a career that will take them off to another company once they have achieved what they wanted with you. Those low-level things like money and conditions will matter more.

How do you find good employees? Don't abandon the method of hiring and vetting that I recommended in the last chapter – using contacts, then introducing them to everyone in the team before you take them on (and giving everyone a veto).

Halsall Associates, a Canadian engineering firm employing upwards of 300 people; maintains two approaches to bring the right people into the fold. The first is to take seriously any employee referrals. From Peter, "Hiring is first and foremost seen as an opportunity for existing employees to identify and recruit people that they know they would want to work with. For employees to succeed, they need to like and trust the people they work with. Making them your key recruiters is one way to make that effective. We financially reward internal recruiting and we publicize the successes. People learn that it works, which reinforces the process."

There is no doubt that the quality of applicant is high when acquired through this method as the employee making the recommendation is placing his or her reputation on the line. In addition, hiring also resembles that of a seedling as it is a process with team involvement. The second preferred method of attraction has been in University Co-op placements. Students, while in University, can work for Halsall for one or more semesters. It provides an opportunity to acquire workplace experience while giving the company a chance to see future prospects in action. Lastly, Halsall runs a parallel process of attracting individuals through advertising and an attractive website, sorting through applications, setting up cold interviews and other big company approaches.

As with Halsall, an HR leader is a must. Its director will set up and run formal structures for recruitment, promotion and training, as well as handling the mechanics of payroll, pensions and so on. They will write a company handbook, which reiterates the mission statement of the company and sets out policies on things like equal opportunity, disciplinary proceedings and other formal processes like how to claim expenses.

How do you hire a good HR person? Ask around. Talk to your mentor or advisory board members, and get them involved in the process. If you must use recruitment professionals, avoid big-name corporate headhunters: find one who really understands SME businesses.

While all this is going on at employee level, your own role in the company will be changing. You are no longer captain of the team, but a director of a large business. Directing a large business is very different from sports captaincy. It's less about flair and humanity, more about rules. Less about motivation, more about strategy. Now is the time to read those management books that talk of business in military terms: big companies are like armies, and their clash is like a war. Step forward two paces, Clausewitz and Sun Zi.

You are not quite as visible as you used to be, walking through the office every day. But you still have to stay positive and occasionally have to put on a big, crowd-pleasing show.

New cornerstones

As I have said, many cornerstones and dream team players (and some entrepreneurs) don't feel at home in the oak world. Or they do feel at home, so much so that they keep working at the rate they did in the first years of the company, and begin to show signs of serious stress: cornerstone burn-out.

Either way, they must be replaced, permanently.

Note that this replacement is *operational*: their place in the *mythology* of the company must remain intact. If a cornerstone wants (or burns) out, keep them as an unsalaried founder director. Insist they take a long, and long-dreamt-of, holiday, or a year out to write that thriller they always talked about (you know, the one about a serial killer in a small software business). When they return, create a leftfield corporate role for them. If they're techies, start a skunkworks. Who knows, they might be like Steve Jobs and turn round and save the company. Maybe they'll be even more like Steve Jobs and do it twice.

If they want to cash in their stake, your first task is to establish a fair valuation for the business. During the dotcom era a useful formula for valuing a business was the number of MBAs in the organization, times the number of incomprehensible buzzwords in the mission statement, times $15 million. To me a business is worth the amount of cash you have in the bank plus the value of the next three months' orders. The truth lies in between, and it is the job of the finance cornerstone to establish this value.

If your finance cornerstone will let you fund the 'loose cornerstone's' exit from cash, that's the best way. If not, talk to the bank.

Resist the temptation to go to the wrong part of town and start hanging out with VCs – you are in a position of weakness, and the best time to talk to these people is when you are very strong.

Finding a good enough replacement is not easy. But it has to be done. Your mentor is a great place to start. They are bound to know some quality people with experience of managing big businesses. Note how the mentor remains important in this phase of the business' life. Mentoring isn't just about starting up: top sportspeople keep coaches long after they have achieved more than the coach ever did. They know that you never stop learning, and that part of learning is to have an excellent teacher.

If your mentor can't come up with anyone, try your own contacts.

Headhunters, as I said, are a last resort. If you do find yourself using this last resort, make sure they don't start acting unethically and stealing people from your rivals. I know this advice may sound goody-goody, but this kind of practice is quietly corrosive to your running of an ethical, effective business, and to the kind of morale and loyalty such a business uniquely commands. You might win a few points in the short term, but it is a loser's strategy over time.

Note that if someone tries that on you it's a signal that (a) you're not managing well enough to keep key staff loyal, and (b) the opposition are getting a bit desperate.

Killing the king

The most difficult person to replace is the entrepreneur, but if you go for growth, it nearly always has to be done some time. Just as parents never really quite see their children as adults – especially when you bring a new partner to meet them and they start telling that story of the time you peed in the wading pool aged 4 – in their heart, the entrepreneur is still king or queen of the dynamic seedling, ready to conquer the world via their Original Beermat.

The kind of erratic, charismatic leadership that got them this far really isn't appropriate any longer, and the cracks nearly always start to show. Examples: they start building a 'praetorian guard', a clique of people loyal to them, not to the company. The guards start doing things in direct contravention of company policy. The entrepreneur's public behaviour becomes bizarre, towards customers or employees.

I'm sure everyone can cite examples of model entrepreneurs who haven't done this – but I have seen it happen so often that you must be prepared for it. It's important not to be judgmental at this time: the entrepreneur is under huge stress. But they are handling the stress disfunctionally, and they must be removed from operational responsibility, or they will drag the business down.

Peter Halsall added to this discussion. "The performance of the "founders" and dream team after a sale will to a large degree determine how the rest adapt. The trust that formed the core of the team must continue in some form. Even if the original leaders leave, they need to demonstrate that everything was done in the best interest of those who are staying. If there are more career opportunities, new processes that increase the chance of success, and a similar team culture, then people will mostly stay. If there are procedures imposed to achieve compliance rather than opportunities, then the people who stay will be the ones appropriate for harvesting an idea, not generating a continuous set of new ideas."

It is, of course, the cornerstones' job to do this, and it is probably one of the hardest things they will ever do. By far the best way is for all four cornerstones to go off-site with the entrepreneur, and *persuade* the entrepreneur that the best thing, for everyone's sake, would be for them to move on.

"Try to see things from the entrepreneur's point of view."

There is no simple way of doing this, but the following hints have proven useful.

- Try to see things from the entrepreneur's point of view. What are their issues, their problems? How can moving on be presented to them as a solution to these issues and problems?
- Don't threaten them. That creates instant conflict and defensiveness. Yes, you have the boardroom power (or should have, if you've built a Beermat company) – but don't flaunt it.

- Don't just comment negatively. The more you can frame the discussion in a positive context – 'Look how far we've come in 10 years' – the better. The 'but ...' that follows will still hurt, of course, but less than a simple diet of rejection.

- Comment on specific behaviours, rather than making a blanket criticism of them as a person. The more the entrepreneur takes it personally, the more defensive they will become. Of course, they will take it personally, but your job is to *minimize* this reaction. You should know them well enough to know when they are going into 'hurt child' mode. Have you said something badly? Stop the conversation at this point and remind them you are not having a hate session aimed at them, but trying to solve a problem.

- Stay in control of yourself. You probably want to let rip after what the entrepreneur has been up to recently, but now is not the time. If they start getting personal with you, don't go down that road. They're upset, remember. Whatever they say, don't hold it against them.

- The entrepreneur must save face. Have a golden escape route ready for them. ('Our CEO is moving on to concentrate on strategic issues as our new president ...') Use your knowledge of them, and your imagination, to design a route which would really appeal to them.

- Be united. Agree among the four of you what the outcomes of the discussion must be.

- Be firm on these outcomes, but have other areas of discussion where the entrepreneur can negotiate *and win*.

These suggestions are not magic formulae, however. This won't be easy or fun. But it's a lot less miserable than a simple show of boardroom voting power and the inevitable backlash. Companies have been destroyed by former leaders who have been insensitively disposed of and who then seek revenge.

If you are the entrepreneur in this situation, go gracefully – while at the same time negotiating the best possible outcome for yourself. Part of you will feel deeply hurt, but don't let that part take over and start a war with the rest of the team. You'll probably feel an overpowering temptation to do something really spiteful to the company and those bastards who have turned round and stabbed you in the back. Resist it.

How do you express your anger normally? A Fender Strat and a stack of Marshall amps? Whacking hell out of a helpless white golf ball? The written word? If you don't think it's too absurd, go and see a therapist and rant and rave at them. Whatever you do, *don't* let your rage loose in your family home, or in your business practice. But don't just lug it around with you, either.

Get negotiating! Once the negotiations are over, make a clean break, during which you treat yourself to something you've always wanted to do but never had time for.

When it's time to go...

➡ **Understand why:**
this is a common experience for successful entrepreneurs

➡ **Negotiate a good exit**

➡ **Handle your anger.** *Let it out in 'safe' ways*

➡ **Make a clean break**
Treat yourself to something fantastic

➡ **Grieve**

➡ **Be proud of what you've done**

➡ **Remember:**
'the best revenge is a happy life'

Give yourself time to get over what amounts to a personal loss, almost like the loss of a loved one. The natural process of grief involves denial, anger, bargaining and, finally, acceptance.

Accept what you have achieved. You have changed the world. You have provided for yourself and your family a standard of living unimaginable to most people on the planet, and beyond the reach of 99 per cent of your compatriots.

Accept that this change was inevitable. Few entrepreneurs make the change from Beermat to corporate boardroom wholly successfully. There is no shame attached to having to go when the time is right. Remember the old adage that 'the best revenge is a happy life'. Get yourself back in balance, enjoying life.

Meanwhile, back at the business, the entrepreneur has to be replaced. This is the time to find an industry professional, skilled in operating a big company. They will bring in new ideas. The company's learning process continues.

As with finding cornerstones, talk to the mentor first and use personal contacts if possible.

Other aspects

Looking at the various other aspects of mighty oak business, rather than just trying to replicate what the management textbooks tell you, I will just make a few observations.

Sales

The sales department was God in the sapling phase, but begins to lose its divinity as the oak grows. The sales department itself becomes more bureaucratized and a lot less fun: sales cornerstones hate sitting behind desks managing sales teams – they want to be out there selling! And a new threat is looming on the horizon: *marketing*. At some point, the growing oak will appoint a marketing director, and, if they are wise, appoint them to the board. Sales and marketing directors should be of equal rank – something the sales cornerstone may find hard to stomach. But stomach it they must.

Advertising may begin to acquire value, as you are aiming at a broader market.

Systems

These become a major issue everywhere. In seedling and sapling companies, the best form of communication was personal contact, plus the odd e-mail or memo. Now communication needs to become formal. As does finance, and, well, everything else, really. In seedling, and even sapling, companies you probably got by with basic word processors and spreadsheets, memory, and pen and paper. Now, you need to develop systematic, formal ways of doing things.

When you are sure of these systematic, formal procedures, yield to one of those people who have been trying to sell you an IT system for the last three years, and *computerize* the procedures. Note that the system must be flexible enough to deal with a manyfold increase in personnel, as that is what you are now aiming for.

Finance

The finance cornerstone will find themselves swamped by the management accounts of a 100-person company. Get a big-company CFO on board.

As regards funding, once you reach that critical mass of around 150 people, and have substantial assets and a good track record, you are now in a position to talk to VCs if you want to. Their risk in providing capital for you is much less than it was at the start, so you can negotiate tough terms with them – terms that keep most of the equity where it belongs, in the hands of the people doing the work. We still recommend getting some extrasharp people on your side if you do go down this route.

Law

I still don't think you should take on lawyers full-time, because the basic principle of 'don't litigate, negotiate' remains constant whatever the size of your company. But clearly the more business you do, the more legal issues are likely to arise. If you only used a small firm at the start, you may need to look for a bigger outfit to advise you, especially when you start doing business overseas (or when you start talking to VCs). Have a stiff drink in hand when their first bill arrives.

Globalization

Don't race into the global marketplace. It's tougher than it looks. Despite a veneer of similarity (McDonald's in Beijing, Kenyan kids in Nike baseball caps, etc.), the world's markets are all very different from one another. So many growing companies have blundered into overseas markets, assuming that if they do it 'like they do at home plus a few tricks learnt off the locals', they'll crack it, but then have lost serious money. Some very big companies, that really should know better, have done this, too.

Please don't throw away all that hard work you've put in by opening 17 offices round the world simultaneously.

"Don't race into the global marketplace. It's tougher than it looks."

However, and this is a moot difference of opinion. The seedling or sapling aspiring to become a mighty oak must factor a global presence as part of the company's growth strategy. While all of the caveats are true, the small firm must start to understand international markets as part of the 'preparing to grow' process.

My tip on going international is 'let the market choose you'. If you suddenly start getting orders from Germany, have a go at the German market. If you secure one big client in an overseas market, set up a tiny office there to service that client, and quietly see what other business you can build up while you're there.

Heading for the exit

Most entrepreneurs and cornerstones take their businesses into the oak stage with some kind of subsequent exit in mind. It keeps them going, in what is essentially an alien environment. 'We'll put up with this big business stuff for three years, then we'll be big enough to get taken over or go public ...'

That exit route is called a *trade sale*. There is usually a compelling commercial logic to trade sales. Most markets begin fragmented, with lots of small players, then begin to coalesce into mature markets, with fewer but bigger players, plus a few boutiques surviving in niches. *You cannot buck this trend.* You have three options:

- grow to be a major player
- get swallowed up by a major player
- lurk in a niche.

Or a fourth: waste time doing nothing, see your customers poached by competitors and go bust.

If a company becomes part of a larger organization, the employees will assume the worst, unless the leadership team is transparent about the reasons for the merger and they are aligned with the interests of the employees. If it is an exit strategy for the leaders, then there should be little surprise if the best talent leaves. If, however, the leaders demonstrate that they are committed to the success of the new entity, and the management of the larger organization demonstrate that they are committed to the culture of the acquired organization, then there is no reason that the trust that was the key inspiration before should not continue.

Initial public offerings (IPOs), or 'floats', are the other major form of exit: 'going public' on the stock exchange. These sound wonderful – all that money, and all that media profile, too! – but behind this glittering surface lurk horrible disadvantages.

One disadvantage is that a sizeable chunk (allow for 10 per cent) of all the value you have carefully built up vanishes one way or other into the pockets of the financial institutions that organize the IPO. Take a walk round your nearest big city financial district and look at the premises these people occupy if you aren't sure whether or not they overcharge for their services.

"You have three options: grow to be a major player, get swallowed up by a major player, or lurk in a niche.**"**

Another is the people you suddenly have breathing down your neck. Institutional shareholders make even VCs look 'long-termist': fund managers get a roasting if their portfolio underperforms for a quarter. And you are also public property in a media sense.

Listing on any exchange tends to involve the company in a web of unfamiliar legal, accounting and reporting rules that do it – and its already hard-pressed staff – no favours.

Share prices are volatile, and their movements are often unrelated to your performance. General levels of market enthusiasm rise and fall, as does the fashionablity of sectors. Just because the financial community has decided that widgets are bad business, you're suddenly at the mercy of all kinds of 'corporate raiders'.

And finally, you don't even get to see that wonderful paper wealth you were credited with the day you 'went public'. There are legal requirements about how long you have to hold stock for – and even when these are satisfied, if you start selling you can set off a market slide. And if the share price has fallen in the meantime ...

I've heard it argued that Public Traded Companies (PTC) or Public Limited Companies (PLC) status adds gravitas to a company. I prefer the gravitas of healthy profits, happy staff and customers, and a reputation for ethical practice.

So what about other exit options? As I've said, a 150-person (or more) company is big enough to talk seriously with VCs, either about a *private sale*, to them, or some kind of *management buy-out*.

Or why exit at all? Why not just stay private?

This option is an excellent one. Not because it makes you megarich, but because private companies can concentrate on what really matters – pleasing their customers – without having to dance to the tune of fund managers, big corporate owners, VCs, stock exchange bureaucrats (etc.). If you think public listing is the inevitable goal for all start-ups, ask massive, world-class and still private companies like Cargill, Mars, Virgin, Bechtel, Levi Strauss ...

Whatever route you follow, it is imperative that the team in charge has thought about the matter and has agreed on its preferred exit. You cannot afford to have disunity on this issue. The best way to avoid disunity is to discuss the issue early on in the oak stage, and to keep revisiting it, not to refuel greed but to ensure everyone knows where they are going. 'So we get big: what then?'

Winning for real

What then, indeed?

Maybe you've got a cheque for a million dollars (or more) in your wallet. You've won!

Sorry, no.

Competing is often a lot easier than really winning. The pop world is full of people who can't handle success, and there are plenty of examples in business, too. I worked with one entrepreneur who later went down a spiral of degeneration ending in death.

This spiral had two strands to it, ironically like the two spiralling strands that create life. One was simple ostentation, beginning with a Ferrari appearing in the business' car park (paid for not out of revenue but from a tranche of funding). The other was abuse of personal power: like many entrepreneurs, this person was manipulative, but he began to get an active kick out of pushing people around. Just how far can you make people jump for money? This soon extended to the sexual area. Allegations of rape were made, then suddenly dropped. At the same time, his consumption mania turned to drugs. Eventually the police got wind of this, and searched his house. Crack cocaine was found, allegedly enough for them to charge him for dealing. He ended up taking two other people for a spin in his latest car and smashing it into a tree. Nobody survived.

"Competing is often a lot easier than really winning."

That's an extreme story, but it happens to be true (and well documented in various media articles, just in case anyone thinks I'm overdramatizing).

Winning is about gaining wealth and power, and about handling their consequences, about not letting them take away your common sense and common kindness.

A myth often propagated by the rich-but-stupid is that they earned their money by lone, solo effort. One against all, Darwinian style. I doubt this is good Darwinism: our ancestors were group animals, not lone hunters like jaguars or eagles. It certainly isn't a good philosophy of business. Who helped you get where you are? Have they shared in the success, too? Winning is about ensuring that the people who helped you win have got something out of the win, too.

The most obvious examples are your fellow founders – but you should all have huge cheques from the sale/IPO or be getting healthy dividends from your private company, so they are not a problem. What about the dream team? They, too, should be in senior positions within a growing organization, so should be happy they teamed up with you. And the people who joined the young oak, employees number 21 to 150? It was these people's reaction to The Instruction Set sale that upset me the most, and I was hugely relieved when most of them quickly adapted to the change and prospered in their new, bigger organization.

I believe in a 'points' system, whereby staff gain points in a pool. This pool can be translated into money on realization of the business' value, by ensuring that a tranche of the proceeds go straight into the pool. This pool is totally transparent – everyone knows what you have to do to get points, and how many points they and everyone else have got.

A working example: if the long-serving receptionist has 1,500 points, and there are 40,000 points in the pool, and the company sells for $10 million, and the rule is that 10 per cent of the proceeds will go to 'point holders', then the receptionist will get $37,500.

What if you stay private? You can still give people shares in the company, but they are less obviously of value – who decides what they are really worth? A generous bonus scheme is probably more appropriate here.

Winning is also about a good night's sleep, about knowing that you haven't stamped on people's faces on the way up. All through this book I have stressed the value of fair, open, ethical dealings with people – with employees, with competition. I believe there is real commercial payoff to this way of doing business, but it also has the benefit of keeping your conscience intact. I also believe that being a winner means putting something back. Spread some good karma. It doesn't have to be actively philanthropic, though if you feel motivated to do this, brilliant.

My own way of doing this was to create a seventies revival band – in one sense, a complete self-indulgence, but I made sure the band was top class, and I've had people come up to me after gigs and say they'd just had the best evening ever. The band was set up to entertain, not to make money, and it showed. It never really did make money: profits just got ploughed back into horn sections, light shows, etc., thus creating work for musicians (who could then go off and create great art if they felt like it) and providing extra entertainment for audiences. And an extra ego-boost for me, of course. But that's the point; the situation was win-win, like all good business practice.

If you'd like to know more about my alter-ego, confused disco legend and seventies fashion guru Mike Fab-Gere, you can find him at www.fabgere.com.

Creating win-win situations is what it has been about all along – from that very first sale. There is a perception that business must be like Buckley's mixture: Tastes bad but it works. This

The Beermat Entrepreneur is a Winner!

➡ Wealth . . .

➡ . . . shared out fairly among everyone who has created that wealth.

➡ A clear conscience.
You fought 'hard but fair'.

➡ Putting something back:
others win, too.

need not be the case and there is plenty of evidence to show that being good is good for business.

In business, it led people to put up with appalling customer relations and appalling industrial relations. In the twenty-first century, neither of these is acceptable. We have to put effort into creating and developing win-win situations, with customers and staff, not just looking after number one and enjoying a good whine when someone gets one over on us.

I wish you every success in your business career. As I've said, now may not look an ideal time to get an enterprise going. But many great businesses have started in hard times (there are more likely to be talented cornerstones with time on their hands, and big business will probably be retrenching, concentrating on core activities and leaving innovation to people like you and me). Follow the patterns I've outlined in this book. Stay positive. And enjoy the journey – and, I hope, the fruits of success.

"Creating win-win situations is what it has been about all along – from that very first sale."

Perhaps my favourite entrepreneur story is of a friend with whom I spent many hours sitting in a pub (where else?) talking about various business plans. He eventually founded a software company, and made a lot of money out of it. We lost contact, but a while ago I got in touch with him and he suggested meeting at that same old pub. We did, and half way through a delicious meal there I commented on how much nicer the old place was. Quiet music, excellent food and drink, and, best of all, a friendly, convivial atmosphere.

'It's improved a lot since I bought it', he explained.

Appendix A

Turning a good idea into a great business: the hurdles

This is not a list of 'things to do' but a list of points at which it is sensible to ratchet up your confidence in an idea's ability to truly make it.

1. The idea sounds special the first time it is mentioned – in the pub.
2. It still sounds great next morning.
3. It sounds even better when some initial work has been done on it.
4. An experienced business person agrees to champion it.
5. Your first customer writes you a cheque.
6. Your first customer is pleased with what the idea has delivered.
7. A founding team of five able individuals commit themselves to realizing the idea.
8. Ten more customers are found.
9. Ten customers are delighted with what the idea has delivered.
10. You pass the five tests (page 96): market belief, sales flow, sound organization, solid finances, people who are ready and eager.
11. You achieve, fairly, the domestic market share aimed for in your Market Conquest Plan.
12. World domination!

cybf.ca

Appendix B

Canadian Youth Business Foundation (CYBF)

As a national organization dedicated to championing tomorrow's entrepreneurs, the Canadian Youth Business Foundation (CYBF) truly understands that Canada's economic prosperity depends on investing in and supporting new and innovative businesses. Included in the support is start-up financing and world-class mentoring. Successful applicants get matched with a mentor – a seasoned business professional from their region, which is a key ingredient for long-term success.

CYBF invests time and money in aspiring entrepreneurs, age 18 to 39, who have a great business idea but find it difficult to obtain financing or mentoring through traditional sources. CYBF delivers its program across Canada through a collaborative network of like-minded organizations called Community Partners. Along with more than 4,000 volunteers, they champion youth entrepreneurship in their communities and directly work with young people to guide them through the entire CYBF process to obtain funding and a mentor.

Founded in 1996, CYBF has invested in more than 5,200 young people, whose businesses have generated millions in sales tax and export revenues, and created more than 20,800 new jobs to date. CYBF is the founder of G20 Young Entrepreneur Summit (G20 YES) and a founding member of the G20 Young Entrepreneurs' Alliance (G20 YEA). The easiest way to get in touch is via their website: www.cybf.ca or their toll-free number 1-866-646-2922.

CYBF offers four fully integrated programs that are built around the 'life cycle' of a young entrepreneur and help to ensure the success of every new start-up.

- Pre-launch coaching – through free, hands-on personal guidance from the Entrepreneur-In-Residence who provides help on a wide variety of topics including, creating a solid business plan or developing financing strategies.

- Online business resources – a robust online Business Resource Centre to service the needs of entrepreneurs, mentors, Community Partners and Local Review Committee Members.

- Financing – CYBF provides start-up financing based on character and a great business idea, with flexible three to five year repayment schedules, and no principal payments in the first year.

- World-class mentoring – highly qualified and dedicated business mentors bring years of experience to young entrepreneurs to encourage them and celebrate their successes. Mentors are hand-matched with every entrepreneur for a minimum of two years to ensure they have support during the critical start-up phase.

CYBF has a positive, down-to-earth approach. If you think you might be eligible, get in touch with them today.

Mentorship perspectives as presented by the Canadian Youth Business Foundation.

CYBF's mentors are experienced business professionals with expertise in areas such as information technology, human resources, marketing, management, finance and business planning, with diverse qualifications and professional designations among others. CYBF mentors are hand-matched with an entrepreneur, committing 4-5 hours per month for a minimum of two years. Through this experience, mentors have an opportunity to build their professional portfolio, have access to business resources and attend various networking events, while providing advice and support to young entrepreneurs in growing their business. CYBF mentoring program is one that proves to be beneficial and rewarding for both the mentor and the entrepreneur.

Appendix C
Recommended reading

We go into the topic of sales – at the heart of the Beermat organization – in greater depth in *Sales on a Beermat* (Random House Business Books, 2008). We recommend everyone reads this book, not just sales people: everyone in an organization (especially if that organization currently consists of one person!) must understand sales and play a part in it.

Finance is another topic that every entrepreneur should understand, even if they have an excellent finance cornerstone. Our guide, *Finance on a Beermat* (Random House Business Books, 2008), which we wrote with two highly experienced SME finance directors, is the best place to go to learn about this.

As you will have worked out reading this book, I do not believe marketing is as important as sales for the start-up. However if you read the above two Beermat guides, complete the trilogy and read Chris' *Marketing on a Beermat* (Random House Business Books, 2008). Much of what Chris calls marketing is what I regard as business common sense, and he avoids the jargon and the corporate focus that disfigure most of the marketing books I see.

High-tech entrepreneurs should read *Crossing the Chasm* by Geoffrey Moore (HarperBusiness, 1999). Actually, all entrepreneurs should give this a read, even if sections of it lose you in details about systems architecture. There is material of huge value for everyone here.

Lovers of strategy should read *The Innovator's Dilemma* by Clayton Christensen (HarperBusiness, 2003). You can take on big business and win!

The E-myth by Michael Gerber is a classic, published in 1985 (see also *The E-Myth Revisited*, HarperCollins, 1995). It's rather Californian in tone – seek your inner entrepreneur! – and, ironically, pushes the message of standardization further than I would push it (unless you want to start a franchise). But it has important things to say about passion, thoroughness and getting the roles right.

Anyone planning to open a restaurant, especially if your ambitions are to scale the business and end up with a chain, should read *Anyone Can Do It* by Sahar Hashemi (Capstone Publishing, 2003). This is an accurate and heartfelt description of the rollercoaster ride that is entrepreneurship.

There are many books on general entrepreneurship – our publisher, Pearson, has a fine list. The best advice is to read as many entrepreneurship books as you can: you'll learn something from all of them. Particular recommendations include *From Acorns ...* by Caspian Woods (Prentice Hall, 2007), *Marketing Judo* by John Barnes and Richard Richardson (Prentice Hall, 2002) and *Think like an Entrepreneur* by Robbie Steinhouse and Chris West (Prentice Hall, 2008). *The New Business Road Test* by John Mullins (Financial Times Prentice Hall, 2005) is an excellent attempt to bridge the gap between the world of the business school and the world inhabited by most entrepreneurs.

Biographies of successful entrepreneurs can be fun and inspiring – but often play up to the 'lone entrepreneur as hero' image. Remember, it's a team game!

Intrapreneurs should bone up on entrepreneurship via the recommendations above, but also read the classic *Intrapreneuring* by Gifford Pinchot (Harper & Row, 1985) and our own *The Boardroom Entrepreneur* (Random House Business Books, 2005).

Finally, do visit our website, www.beermat.biz, for the latest Beermat articles and ideas.

In addition to the excellent recommendations offered by the authors I would like to add a couple of books that have been useful as guides and sources of inspiration for students launching businesses or pursuing an entrepreneurial lifestyle.

Disciplined creativity is explained and demonstrated in the book, "Think Better" by Tim Hurson.

Another creativity enabler comes from, "The Innovative Team" by Chris Grivas and Gerard Puccio.

I also enjoy books that broader my perspective. "The Goal" by Eliyahu Goldratt was a different read. I also believe books that make sense of things like economics are of value. To this, "Executive Economics" by Shlomo Maital made me understand that economics was a valuable tool for business decision making (and not a series of graphs with little meaning).

I still find value in books related to strategy. Henry Mintzberg and Peter Drucker remain at the top of my list.

The most important thing is to be receptive to learning. Don't make it a practice — make it a way of life. Allow yourself to be challenged and to grow. It has an impressive impact on your leadership and the culture of your firm.